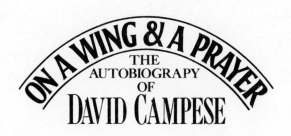

ON A WING & A PRAYER
THE AUTOBIOGRAPY OF
DAVID CAMPESE

To Ben

I hope that you enjoyed
that sport Soccer. Now you should
play the Bo5 game in the world.
And maybe you to can play
for the Wallabies ha ha! sorry
Kevin

Best Wishes

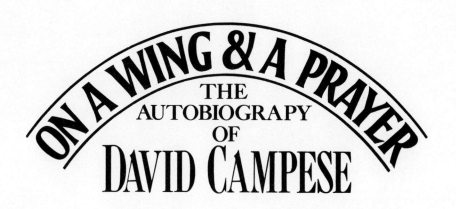

ON A WING & A PRAYER
THE AUTOBIOGRAPY
OF
DAVID CAMPESE

DAVID CAMPESE
WITH PETER BILLS

Macdonald
Queen Anne Press

A QUEEN ANNE PRESS BOOK

© David Campese 1991
First published in Great Britain in 1991 by
Queen Anne Press, a division of
Macdonald & Co (Publishers) Ltd
Orbit House
1 New Fetter Lane
London EC4A 1AR

A member of the Maxwell Macmillan Pergamon Publishing Corporation

Design: Peter Champion

A CIP catalogue record for this book is available from the British Library

ISBN 0-356-17958-3

Typeset by Cylinder Typesetting Limited, London

Printed in Great Britain by
Butler & Tanner Ltd, Frome and London

CONTENTS

ACKNOWLEDGEMENTS

Through a couple of northern hemisphere winters and some typically tough winter days in Sydney in the southern hemisphere (how can you call warm sunshine, 17 degrees and people swimming off Coogee Beach wintertime?) this book was compiled with much care, and above all, enjoyment by Campo and myself. We hope it gives you as much pleasure reading it as we had putting it together.

In deep mid-winter in Kent, we were fortified by a steady supply of coffee and biscuits, not to say luscious meals, from Averil, my long-suffering wife. Across the world in Sydney, I lived the life of Reilly at Simon Poidevin's elegant home overlooking the ocean, and my gratitude to him, as well as to his brother Andy and wife, Anna, is endless. And, finally, in Milan (once I had dragged the subject kicking and screaming from his bed each morning), we completed the final text.

Perhaps the biographer of Jean-Pierre Rives ought to have been prepared, but if that splendid Frenchman was thought to be laid-back, then this remarkable Australian of whom you are about to read could perhaps best be described as horizontal. Not too much disturbs Campo from his measured lifestyle, but having someone pounding the keys of a computer in his apartment before nine o'clock in the morning was clearly a far more intimidating prospect than facing any All Black.

Also in Sydney, Daryl and Julie MacGraw were sage counsellors. In Italy, Vittorio Munari, who considers Campo to be more like a brother than a friend, offered some interesting thoughts, and Mark Ella and his wife, Kim, read the manuscript assiduously and were equally helpful. As for Campo himself, he wishes to apologise to (sorry, he said thank) all his team-mates over the years!

Finally, we would like to acknowledge the assistance of CSI Limited, the television sports distribution company, without whom this book would not have been realised. We would also like to thank Caroline North, Publishing Director of Queen Anne Press, for taking on the book, editing it and seeing it through to fruition; Peter Champion for the design, Oscar Heini for the production, Kate Truman for proofreading and Linda Silverman for her help in obtaining photographs.

As to why Campo asked an Englishman, traditionally an Aussie's greatest foe, to help him put his book together, I am at a complete loss to understand. You had better ask him. Perhaps he just felt sorry for me after what the Australians have done to the English cricket team over several years. However, our friendship, forged in some thoroughly unlikely and glittering world locations such as Dunedin, seems to have survived this painful process, which just goes to show that those Englishmen who stuck a pin in the world map in 1787 and decided to choose Australia as the overseas holiday destination of the future perhaps knew a thing or two more than they were willing to admit at the time.

Peter Bills
July 1991

FOREWORD

FROM SERGE BLANCO
CAPTAIN OF FRANCE

Perfect rugby is impossible to define because everyone will have their own set of criteria. Some people like a particular style, others prefer the traditional game, or quite simply, efficiency. But rugby is in the lucky position of having men who live the game with passion, commitment and, above all, love. The pleasures that are derived from working as a team are immense and rugby is the only sport which gives men of very different physiques the opportunity to play a role in matches which will be forever engraved on people's memories.

Each has his part to play, but sadly not all the members of the team will receive due recognition for the work they have contributed. A forward will often be overlooked when it comes to distributing the prizes, and yet it is important to realise that the greatest tributes will be paid to him by the threequarters, who would be nothing without him. It is also true to say that, seven times out of ten, the backs provide the finish as well as the spectacular movements, but they can just as easily be creative.

David Campese is the most exciting example of these threequarters; he is the epitome of the modern player. The magician of Australian rugby has shown us a thousand turns, all as beautiful as one another. He never lacks spirit or commitment in a game, and manages to inspire team-mates and opponents alike with his enthusiasm.

He will leave his mark on world rugby and is an example to young players everywhere. I am proud to have played against him and have only one regret – that we have not had the opportunity to share our enjoyment of the game wearing the same jersey.

Mon cher David, thank you for your love of the game, and above all for the respect your name evokes in rugby in France and around the world.

Au revoir mon ami!

CHAPTER
—1—

A CALL TO CHANGE MY LIFE

In that short, abbreviated hour between the fading of the winter's afternoon sun and the onset of that bitter night cold which persuades me that I could never live in the British Isles, I turned over in bed at the Surrey hotel where I was staying to take a telephone call which was to offer me the chance to change my life forever. The telephone had broken only a light sleep. It is not unusual for sportsmen to get an hour or two resting on their beds at the end of a day on tour. You have probably completed a full training session in the morning and then spent perhaps an hour or two working out in the gymnasium in the afternoon. Physical exercise can be pretty exacting and it is never a bad idea to rest up for a while before heading down for dinner wherever you happen to be staying.

Telephone calls to the players are a regular part of touring. It could have been from a journalist, seeking some thoughts on a forthcoming match, perhaps from a contact we had met on the tour or even someone calling us up from back home, although the fact that it was the middle of the night by this time in Australia made that less likely. We were preparing for the penultimate match of the tour of England and Scotland by the 1988 Australian Wallabies. But the voice on the other end of the line certainly was not trying to find out what I thought might happen in the match against the Combined Services the next day at Aldershot!

My room-mate handed me the telephone and the accent I heard immediately ended any thoughts of the call being from home. In fact, it was one unknown to me until the caller identified himself as an official of the St Helens Rugby League club. That gave me a clue as to what the call might be about. I had heard of St Helens long ago in the days when I played

Rugby League back in Australia at junior level. Their name had been associated more recently with a great Australian Rugby League star, Mal Meninga. The big Queenslander had made such an impact when he joined the club for a season in the 1980s that he became something of a legend in that part of the north. They couldn't get enough of Mal Meninga around St Helens way, which showed that the old idea that every Pom loathed every Aussie was a bit wide of the mark. It must have been just every other one!

More recently, the successful association between St Helens and Australian players had been extended by Michael O'Connor. The club thought so much of Mick that they once flew him over specially from Sydney to London just to play a single match in an English Cup final. That spoke volumes of their estimation of his abilities, and they were not wrong. I had played both with and against Mick O'Connor in the early years of my career because he, like me, came originally from the Australian Capital Territory state and we knew of each other at schoolboy level. Mick was a superb Rugby Union player, full of skill, vision, speed and class. He could kick goals and score tries and his ability made plenty of other scores for those around him. When he went to League, joining the St George's club in Sydney, Rugby Union lost a terrific performer. His career in League blossomed equally well. He went on not only to play for the Kangaroos, but to make a big impression in the Test side. It transpired that St Helens had done their homework on me, because they had asked O'Connor if there was anyone he would recommend. I was impressed by the fact that they had taken the trouble to talk to him before settling on a player they wanted. That suggested a professional club willing to do the spadework so necessary to conclude a major signing.

I asked the St Helens official what was involved. His reply made me sit bolt upright in bed. I was told the overall deal was worth between £300,000 and £350,000 ($660,000 and $770,000) to me over three years, dependent upon a few variables such as number of appearances. I suppose there was a slight pause in my reply. In those few seconds, a lot of thoughts went through my mind. The memories of home, of my childhood, of our regular shortage of dollars . . . and of the sum of around three-quarters of a million dollars which this rugby club had just offered me to join them.

You cannot make decisions of that magnitude on the telephone. I pleaded my present preoccupation with the tour, which was true, for although I was not playing the next day against the Combined Services, we had the match against the Barbarians to plan for when we reached Cardiff two days later. So I put the phone down, and I think that within five minutes, perhaps less time, I had decided against the deal.

I would like to say it was nothing to do with St Helens. They did everything professionally and properly, and they were not to back off easily after the initial approach had been made. But my mind was made up at a very early stage. And, conversely, my decision had everything to do with money. For me, life is about a great many things before money comes into the equation. Sure, you cannot get too far without it, and I have firm views on the way players in Rugby Union have been manipulated by and for the benefit of the authorities but to their own great loss.

Money is interesting – it has to be to anybody who is not a millionaire – and some might think that because of the circumstances of my upbringing it would influence every decision I make. We never had much spare cash in my family, but despite that, I have always felt that enjoyment of life was far more important. I have always been more interested in playing Rugby Union than making a financial killing by going to League. The proposed St Helens deal was spread over three years. It would have worked out at around £110,000 ($275,000) a year, give or take a few thousand. That is big money, but it would have meant living in England throughout the northern hemisphere winter. I was not at all keen on that side of the equation. I didn't know exactly where St Helens was, but I knew enough to realise I would be in for a cold, grey winter, month after month of it, if I signed to play Rugby League in England. When you are far from home, the one thing you want is to be happy with your surroundings: I somehow doubted that I would be deliriously happy to find myself in a flat in St Helens.

Whether St Helens knew it or not, I don't know, but their offer was not the first I had received to turn professional. Approaches came as soon as I got home after my first-ever overseas tour with the Wallabies, the 1982 trip to New Zealand. I won my first cap over there against the All Blacks, and immediately I got back, clubs started ringing up asking if I wanted to play League. Several Sydney League clubs made contact – Canberra Raiders, Manly-Warringah, Canterbury and, when they first joined the League, The Gold Coast – but I told them I wasn't ready. It was always left that I would give them a call when I was. I never called any of them back.

I think what I saw of League guys when I was young put me off the game for life in terms of my possible involvement in it. Don't get me wrong, I love watching League and often go to see it live. The game has some marvellous footballers who possess great skills. But when I was a kid in Queanbeyan, ACT, I played League and got fed up with constantly being abused because I missed tackles. I was not the greatest tackler in the world, and some say I'm still not crash-hot at that part of the game. But in League you have to make every single tackle because if you don't, the chances are the opposition will score as a result. My chief problem on this front came in the last League game I can remember playing. It was an Under-16 match, for Queanbeyan Blues against Belconnon, one of the local teams. I was a lot skinnier than I am now and I was really scared of tackling.

I played in that Grand Final, missed a tackle or two and they blamed me for it. I guess I was a sensitive guy, I still am really, and although I have always taken stick in my life, in those days I really didn't know how to handle it. Consequently, I took it much harder than would be the case today and I think that experience put me off League.

I had always had trouble with my tackling. But a friend who used to play Union, David Grimmond, began to help me in the tuition of my sprint training, and when I started to play Rugby Union, he was also the one who taught me how to tackle. David was a great tackler and I learned a lot from him. I came to understand that it was really just a matter of confidence. In League, no one had bothered to show me how to tackle properly and therefore I had had no confidence at all in the tackles I did attempt.

Also, I saw too many of my friends who played League drink far too much for my liking. In Union they had been super players, but the biff-bang of League and the grog which is associated with it turned me off. I saw too many throw their careers away. When I was 16 the coach of our League side, Steve Hewson, would have parties and everybody would be drinking beer. You know how it is, kids out on their own at 15 or 16 like to play the macho-man role, thinking themselves ever so clever if they can hold a pint and swill it. But I was never much impressed with that idea then, nor am I now. Consequently, I always found myself alone drinking orange juice, because I didn't drink alcohol, against a background of everyone else getting steadily drunk and I didn't fit into the picture terribly well. But I had no intention of joining in because I wanted to achieve something in my sporting life, and I didn't see alcoholic binges as the best path towards that. I wanted to succeed in rugby and it was around that time, having seen what a League side was like, that I made the decision to play Union. It seemed to me that in League teams there was more time put into drinking and smoking than in Union. There was no pressure from the coaches or administrators on the kids to give up these habits, and I thought 'What are these guys doing?' But I realised I had to get on with what I wanted to do and that that part of any sport didn't interest me.

There was also the point that at that age I didn't think League looked a great game to play at professional level. I believe that in Rugby Union you can really enjoy yourself when you go out on to the field. I always try to do that, and hope that my colleagues go on to the paddock with the same attitude. Sure, winning is very important. But if you come in from a game you have lost and you have not had any pleasure from the 80 minutes, then what has been the point of it all? In an amateur sport, enjoyment must be the main reason for involvement because there cannot be a great deal else. But in League, there was so much pressure. One coach once told me after I had missed a tackle that if I missed another, he would take me off the field even if it meant playing on with only 12 guys. I regard that kind of pressure as unacceptable for any 14-year-old.

League players earn big money, but how could they honestly say they enjoy it? When they are playing, they belt each other so hard that after they have finished they are too tired to do anything except go back to the club and drink. OK, a lot of people still do that in Union but the amateur game's greatest attribute is that you can still have a laugh with your mates when you are on the field. I don't believe that attitude is possible in top-line Rugby League. You try to enjoy yourself a lot more in Union, sometimes even sharing a joke with an opponent. To me, however, if someone is paying you, the fun side disappears. It becomes a business and is taken far too seriously. It is your job, what you get paid for, and the scope for humour disappears. If you do something wrong in Union, it doesn't mean you get dropped the next week. But it could well do in League. You are out there only to win.

Essentially, deciding whether to accept the carrot which continues to be dangled in front of an increasing number of Rugby Union players is a very private and personal decision. And I have no problem accepting the views of those who wish to take up such approaches. I talked with Andrew Leeds, the Wallaby full-back, shortly before he signed professional forms with Parramatta, and he told me what was on offer. I just told him it was his decision and he had to do what suited him best. The only thing I question is how many players around the world have gone into League solely and simply for the money. A friend of mine told me he had spoken to one ex-Wales international who had obviously not been enjoying life in professional rugby. But he had to go on because he had another four years three months left to do on his contract: obviously, he had not gone there principally to achieve something in League, but mainly for the money. If I had ever gone to League, do not doubt that money would have been a factor. But never the only one. I would have wanted to play Test rugby in League and nothing short of that would have satisfied me. And then, if I had reached the Kangaroo side, I would have wanted to stay there and to have been considered in time one of the best-ever players the game had known. That is my way: I seek high standards and I am never happy if I fall short of them.

I just wonder whether in a country like Wales, where many players have gone to the big Rugby League clubs in the north of England in recent times, they could honestly say they turned professional for the challenge or because they wanted to live in places like Hull and Widnes. I somehow doubt it. I should think that money was the only real reason for the majority of players going, and I don't believe that is the best background for entering the professional game.

After their first approach to me, St Helens persisted. After the Wallaby tour had concluded at Cardiff, they kept on ringing me in Italy, where I had gone on to play. And when I finally got home to Australia, they rang me there, too. They offered to fly me over to London to watch the Cup final in which they were playing that year. I hedged and put them off, which was bad on my part, really, because I had made my decision. I listened to them but had no real intention of going through with it. The saga drifted on until the night after the final Test match between Australia and the British Lions in Sydney on 15 July 1989. It was a disastrous match for me personally, and afterwards I just went home. I was at the home of my friends Daryl and Julie when St Helens caught up with me. They asked Daryl: 'Will he come?'. Daryl promptly said no. Then, incredibly, and quite beyond my expectation, they immediately offered more money – another £10,000 (around $21,000 at that time) – but the answer remained the same. I suppose I was shocked that the interest from St Helens was still there after my performance that day. But perhaps they figured I would be an easy target after a game like that!

At the time of writing, I can honestly say that there is no offer which would tempt me to go to Rugby League. I think St Helens finally realised that, once I had rejected their second offer. If someone rang and offered me a million dollars, I would not be interested. They say every man has his price, but you can leave me out of that generalisation because if I wasn't perfectly happy with the idea, no amount of money on earth would tempt me to do it. Call me a bit odd, if you wish. But maybe, just maybe, if you don't have very much money when you are young, then you don't miss it.

There is only one aspect of Rugby League of which I am envious and that is all the interest and publicity the sport generates in Australia in comparison with Rugby Union. Being a Union player, I find that both sad and disappointing. Sometimes, even before a Rugby Union Test match at home, it is hard to find any proper advance notice of the game in the press because officials in Rugby Union hardly bother to advertise matches. Now whether that is simply because the ARU does not possess the financial resources or whether they do not think it is necessary, I don't know. Perhaps they don't even know how. But I do know that the game is suffering as a result.

I want to state here and now that I do not doubt the sincerity of the guys involved in the ARU. I think they are probably all extremely honest, decent people, but I don't believe they are putting Union into the market-place, which needs to happen if we are to survive and prosper in a battle with League. Certainly in New South Wales, and particularly the Sydney newspapers, League is massive by any other standards. It dwarfs all other winter sports, filling columns of pages every single day in both the morning and evening papers. Open a newspaper and you see League all over its sports pages; turn on the television, and live League games are being shown regularly. You can see a Friday night game live, a Sunday game on delayed telecast at around 6.00 pm that evening and then regular interviews and news stories throughout the week. That represents the kind of blanket coverage Rugby Union can only dream about, and the long-term portents for the amateur code disturb me. Any sport must promote itself; that is as elementary as ABC. If it does not, then it risks drifting out of the hearts and minds of those floating sports fans who might very well turn up at an event if it is presented to them in a sufficiently bright, inventive manner. But in this respect, Union is losing the battle with League and that must concern everyone connected with the game.

It is quite possible that all this has something to do with the type of people generally associated with the amateur code, those who go to Union games. Certainly, as a generalisation, they are not terribly demonstrative: they don't get up in the crowd and roar at their team or the opposition. The referee, maybe, but not the players! My former fiancée, Cindy, and Mark Ella's wife, Kim, once went to see a Test match at the Sydney Cricket Ground and when the teams came out, they stood up and shouted for Australia. Half-a-dozen people near them glowered and told them to be quiet and sit down. In a country which has a reputation for 'fronting up', as we like to say, and for cheering on the team you support, this was unbelievable.

You only have to fly across the Tasman Sea to experience the difference in another part of the southern hemisphere – New Zealand. No one cares about anything there except supporting the All Blacks. Test matches are discussed by farmers, city accountants, housewives, hotel cleaning women and young children. The whole country gets behind their team and when the New Zealand side actually walks out on to a Test arena to play a game the crowd roars its support. As an Australian, I just wish my fellow countrymen made that sort of noise when the Wallabies played a Test. They clap when you walk out and walk off but not much more. This is strange, because we Australians are not naturally quiet, reclusive, withdrawn people. But go to a Rugby Union match and it certainly starts to look that way.

Rugby Union is a marvellous game and where it scores over League, in my book, is in the freedom players have to express themselves. You simply cannot play League purely for the fun and pleasure; too much is at stake. Union is different. It has its serious side – facing the All Blacks when you are two down in a three-match series and trying desperately to avoid a whitewash is fairly severe business. That was the situation facing the Wallabies in August 1990, and I am pleased to say that we won that match and ended our tour of that year with a better look to the whole trip. But a month or six weeks later, three Wallaby players, Nick Farr-Jones, Michael Lynagh and myself, as well as Stephen Cutler, were flying across the world to London to represent the Barbarians in their Centenary games against England and Wales. That was the fun side of our game; the chance to play a match which was a test of skills but also an entertainment without the pressure of acquiring points for a victory. Rugby Union ought to treasure that quality because, in my view, it remains *the* special feature of the sport. If the game ever becomes purely a question of winning league matches to acquire points and finish the season at the head of a championship table, then it will lose an enormous amount of its intrinsic appeal.

It is the view, I think, of a majority of players that there is often too great a gulf in views and attitudes between those who administer the game and those who actually play it. I certainly hold this opinion. In perhaps too many cases, the players wonder just what sort of thought process has gone into the decisions taken by the people in charge of the game. 'He is out of touch with the modern world' is a phrase used all too often to describe certain leading officials in the world of Rugby Union, and that is a pity.

When that big offer came from St Helens, I admit that the memory of certain incidents in which those involved in committees made ridiculous decisions went through my mind. As a player, you come up against quite a few of this kind of decision. You wonder who framed laws which allow them and you ponder the modern-day awareness of those presiding over and trying to defend such antiquated rules. Nevertheless, I still believe that Rugby Union is basically a better game to be in, and I also think that there is more opportunity to earn money through Rugby Union than League. I had better explain what I mean by that remark!

It is simply that a whole world of business contacts and opportunities opens up to the successful rugby player in his country. It does not matter whether you are talking about Wales, Australia, Ireland or Argentina – who can honestly say that they have not enjoyed certain perks which have come about due to their association with the game? It is seen, to anyone who wants to look hard enough, in club rugby all over the world. Major clubs in England and Wales recruit the best players because they are able to provide help with employment which will, inevitably, include a nice motor car. If an official at a top club knows someone in a successful business, he will use his contacts to line up a job for a particular player. Now I see nothing wrong with that, and it happens the world over. But it becomes a controversial subject because under the century-old regulations of the amateur game, technically no player shall be allowed to receive an inducement for playing. And yet these rules are being broken all over the world, with perks for playing thoroughly apparent in virtually every country. If that, therefore, is not a bad law I do not know what is.

In the amateur game of Rugby Union, you should be treated a lot better than in League, but the reality is far from ideal. I have long since lost count of the number of cramped, uncomfortable airline journeys I have made squashed up in economy class at the back of a plane while officials from the IRB, for example, and from the individual unions travel in first class or, at worst, business class. There has been, it is fair to say, some progress on this front in more recent times: we did fly business class when we went to Britain for the Barbarians Centenary matches. But even then, although the Barbarians invited the wives of the Australian players selected for those games to accompany their husbands to London, the players had to pay to fly them over.

But, as I have said, Rugby Union should chiefly be about enjoyment. We all whinge about certain aspects of the game at times, and certain things do stick in your throat, some of which I have already mentioned, but when all is said and done, ask me which game I would prefer to be in and my answer is written in the long list of matches I have played for the Wallabies. For me, the pleasure is in going out in front of 50,000 people and doing something that no other player can do. Really entertaining and thrilling the crowd – that is what I love to do. When you are young, you just want to get out on to the paddock, play the game and have a good time. Whoever is in front of you, you just want to beat that person.

Eight years on down the track, I have established a reputation and now people expect me to conjure a spectacle all the time. The trouble is that when you don't they call you a failure! In the 1989 Grand Final for Randwick, every time I got the ball, I could hear people shouting their expectations. They were just waiting for me to do something. Believe me, in 1990 we missed Mark Ella, because he had far more ability to do brilliant things on the field than I ever had.

My rugby philosophy is that you should always come off the field knowing that you have done your absolute best. You must be satisfied that in almost every given situation, you have tried your utmost to do something special to help your team win the game. No one goes on to a field to lose a game or to play superbly himself even if his team ends up losing. Entertaining the crowd comes high on my personal list of ambitions, but for a long time now I have felt it essential that all this is achieved within the context of the team. Who wants to walk off the field having scored two or three tries, knowing that your team lost the match? The individual tries count for nothing in that situation. Rugby is a team game and it is about 15 guys working together to succeed. I freely admit that when I was younger, I did not necessarily hold such views. Some people have told me I was too selfish, too preoccupied with trying to make a name for myself rather than helping the team and I am quite prepared to accept that criticism. Some of my mates have told me that, including Mark Ella. They know; you can expect to be told the truth by such people. And I am sure it was so when I was younger. I am glad to say that nowadays I think the success of the team is far more important than that of any particular individual. From the touchlines, it might very well seem as though I play as an individual, but that is not the way I regard myself. I cannot afford to be that way on the field in a team sport. For the top-line golfer, an entirely selfish attitude is perfectly understandable, even desirable. How else could you achieve that level of personal motivation for continuing success but by shutting out of your mind every other thought and every other person? It has to be the way to do it. But rugby is different.

Even in a social match, something like a game for the Australian or British Barbarians, you have to be mindful of the presence and wishes of those players around you. I don't advocate individualism as a general policy to any rugby player, but at the same time, I do demand the right to think for myself. If you take that away from every player, you are left with no opportunity to achieve the unexpected. To have players thinking differently has to be the way of a team, even if the basic game plan is adhered to. But you cannot expect to extinguish every ounce of individuality in a team and then see it go out and play not only attractive rugby but a winning game. I am firmly in favour of allowing, and indeed encouraging, players to make their own decisions out on the field. I think the influence of the coach has become too powerful in a great many cases these days. You hear coaches laying down the law about anything and everything and then complaining when the team loses. That is crazy because if you take away a player's ability to make his own decisions, he will be incapable of achievement on the field in any situation which demands the slightest amount of thought.

That may have been another major reason for my rejection of every overture from Rugby League. My whole life, my approach to every day, is to have a free perspective; a freedom which no one can take away. It does not mean a blank cheque to do ridiculous things but to me, it is important to have that basic freedom because it is what I have always sought. The idea of having someone telling me I have to be at this training ground at that particular time every single day, or telling me what I should or should not be doing when I get the ball and how I have been doing it wrong for all these years, disturbs me. I suspect that that could have happened had I gone to professional rugby. For the orthodox, disciplined person it would have presented no problem. He would have adapted smoothly. But I cannot say I am that person; I love my freedom, my ability to make decisions on whatever aspect of life confronts me. So it could have been the wrong move to make.

It has to be said that I am far from a conventional figure whether you are talking about life as a whole or rugby in particular. My life would be a nightmare for a lot of people, I suppose, living in different countries for long periods of the year. Perhaps others could not accept the loneliness which can be a part of my life; maybe they would be driven mad by the lack of security which I guess is the price I pay for not having a more conventional life or job. But each to his own, and I can say with total honesty that it suits me well enough. In all things you encounter highs and lows, and I am probably more prone to both than most people because I am unorthodox, especially on the rugby field. Just ask my mates, who have had plenty of cause to curse me at various times during my career! But the old Sinatra song comes back to me: 'I did it my way', and I have no regrets at all about that when I look back and reflect upon my playing career and life in general.

Three-quarters of a million dollars? Maybe one day at some point in the distant future, I will look back at that and wonder what it might have meant to me. But I very much doubt whether I shall ever regret taking the decision I did. Rugby is my life: a hobby, yes, but a life-consuming one. Involvement in this game gives you so much opportunity and the chance to have years of fun. You see the world, meet some fascinating people and make lifelong friends. What more could you ask for? The most fun I have ever had has been playing alongside the Ella brothers, especially Mark, because we thought alike and were on almost identical wavelengths. Whenever we went out on to a rugby field, we wanted to have a good time and enjoy ourselves; win, too, of course, but never to the total detriment of our enjoyment. After all, isn't that what rugby is supposed to be about? It gets heated and occasionally it gets heavy, and Mark is just one of the people who has had a go at me for making mistakes. That is fair enough – no one is perfect and it doesn't do any harm to be reminded where you went wrong.

But the ultimate pleasure is in playing the running game, the competition with friends and the sharing of great experiences on and off the field. The laughs, the humour and the stories all combine to make Rugby Union what it is: a special game devoid of the pressures financial considerations induce when they get a hold on a sport. Had I gone to St Helens or Canberra Raiders or some such club, a great portion of my love for sport might have died.

Lasting happiness is not a commodity money can buy, unfortunately. I know a lot of friends who have a great deal of money but I could not call them happy. They seem to spend much of their lives fighting each other over money or problems arising from the wealth which was supposed to be creating the happiness. Of course, everyone needs security for the future, perhaps me more than most, for when rugby is finished for me, I have no predetermined path to tread. One day I shall have to try and find another career because I do not have anything apart from rugby at the moment. For others, it is different. For my mate Nick Farr-Jones ('Skippy'), the guy who has become the closest to me since Mark Ella's retirement in understanding what makes me tick and how to react to it, life is assured in a business sense. Nick has spent years training to be a solicitor and will take up that profession with even greater dedication when rugby no longer occupies such a large part of his life. For me it is quite different.

My whole philosophy of life is geared to the belief that you take your chances, making the most of them when they come along. You only live once, so make the most of your life while you have it. But Nick and I are different guys. Nick's life is altogether more conventional, more organised than mine will probably ever be. I live my life as I play my rugby, always looking for enjoyment, an immediate pleasure from it all. I don't look far into the future and never have done. Call that a weakness, a mistake if you wish, but it has never been my way to lay plans for ten or 20 years hence. It's fine for those who are happier that way, but it's not my kind of style. When I finish playing, I shall just have to hope that some kind businessman fancies giving a job to a beaten-up, slowed down, has-been rugby player, because if no one does, I don't know what will fill my life. Optimism, however, has always been one of my traits and I shall continue to believe in that quality until such time as fate decrees otherwise.

St Helens made me a marvellous offer which would have removed all financial uncertainties for the remainder of my life, had I invested it carefully and not blown the lot on fast cars and even faster women, and there was not a great deal of danger of that happening! But somehow, even an offer that size was not big enough to tempt me to give up so much. And that is why I say there is probably no offer on earth which would persuade me to take the road to Rugby League. My love for Rugby Union goes deep. It is a game which has great traditions and creates a worldwide network of friends and alliances. The times may be changing, and Rugby Union is going to have to abandon some of its century-old traditions, a fact which has dawned only slowly upon many of those who administer the game. But change it will, to reflect the times in which we live. And at the end of that process of alteration, I very much doubt whether the basic pleasures of the game will have been damaged. Friendships will continue to be forged from association with the game; the pleasure of playing will not be impaired. How can it be, simply by a player earning a few hundred dollars from an after-dinner speaking engagement? Too much nonsense has been spoken and written about the perils of the game coming into the modern world. Rugby is great; it will survive. There might be less hypocrisy in it, but that will be no bad thing. By clinging to archaic rules, the administrators have forced a certain degree of cynicism to creep into the game, and for that they must accept responsibility. A law regarded as universally bad cannot command respect; rugby is no different to the road in that sense.

Rugby will probably endure forever because young guys will always want a pursuit in which they can have fun and companionship, playing a sport alongside their mates. I believe in that formula because it was the one I chose when St Helens came along. I have no reason to express the slightest regret at the decision I took.

CHAPTER
2

THE LONELINESS OF THE LONG-DISTANCE RUGBY-PLAYER

Not very long after the 1988 Wallabies had completed their tour of England and Scotland, a film producer working for CSI, a London television sports distribution company with an association with the ARU, flew out to Italy to talk to me, at some length, about the possibility of making a programme on my rugby-playing life. Initially, this intrigued me. There were plenty of other rugby players in the world before me and doubtless there will be just as many after I have retired and been forgotten. But what interested the guy from the film world, or so he told me, was the fact that my life revolved utterly and completely around rugby. He seemed to think that I was one of the first of a new breed – the 24-hour-a-day, 12-months-of-the-year, full-time Rugby Union player. His belief was that this was a trend which would gain in popularity among the leading players in the game. And that set me thinking.

Will players really devote themselves totally to the game, to the exclusion of all other interests? Peering into a crystal ball and foretelling the future of rugby seems about as easy as forecasting the result of the three o'clock race at Randwick. In fact, you would probably have more chance of sorting out the form and forecasting with greater accuracy the outcome of a horse race. In that world, there are clear pointers, reliable evidence to hand on previous trends and results. Rugby Union is notoriously difficult to understand in terms of the administrators' likely future policy. At the end of the 1970s, those in charge of the game in the northern hemisphere stated most emphatically that they did not want a World Cup and therefore there would never be one. Lo and behold, in 1987, Rugby Union's first-ever World Cup was held.

Comparatively late in the 1980s, the secretary of the English Rugby Union, Dudley Wood, was saying that there could be no question of manipulating the rules to allow players to profit in any financial way from the playing of the game. Yet by 1990, the English had moved enough to allow some limited opportunity for players within the game to earn money from activities outside the sport, such as the writing of books and newspaper articles and public speaking. So, as you can see, rugby does not have a very consistent track record on these topics. On the subject of the English, I was disturbed to hear that several of the English players had refused to attend a dinner staged by Save and Prosper, a London finance company which is the major sponsor of the English Rugby Union. I believe they wouldn't go because the question of payment for personal appearances had not yet been settled in negotiations between the people at Twickenham and the players. To me, it is disgusting for players to expect money from the sponsor of the English Rugby Union to attend a dinner. If you are a player, you should go to a dinner like that. I am the first to say players should get something out of the game, but in that case I have no hesitation in saying that the English players who pulled out were wrong. It looks as though the English players have got pound signs in both eyes, which means they have gone totally overboard from getting nothing to wanting everything.

Coming back to myself, I think it is probably correct to say that I was one of the first players in the world to take up the game for 12 months of the year. To be able to do that, of course, you have to play six months in one hemisphere and six in the other, and I am delighted that I have been able to do that through my connection with Italy, which is a genuinely close one in my family. I can still remember some of my life as a very young child in Italy before my family moved back to Australia. Given this link by my family name, I am qualified to play rugby for Italy, if I so desire, and therefore I think it is only fair that I am allowed to play half my rugby in that country.

The idea that Australian or New Zealand players should be able to complete their own domestic season and then travel across the world to represent another club in another country, tours by their own national team permitting, is one which I have no difficulty accommodating. It seems to me that the world is the oyster of the young sportsman today. He can travel more easily than ever before, reach far-flung places quicker than has ever been known in history and develop his learning and understanding of different people and foreign cultures better than was once ever imagined. Ask generations of Australians or New Zealanders where they really learned most about life and I am willing to bet the vast majority would give the same answer: from overseas travel. The experience of travelling alone or with a mate or two is second to none; you grow up almost overnight and fill your memory with a vast bank of knowledge and information from personal experience. You can read history and textbooks until you are cross-eyed but nothing can equal the experience, the thrill of seeing things first-hand.

I remember travelling in a car once in some part of the South of France, during the Wallaby tour of that country in 1989. We had the best possible guide in Peter FitzSimons, one of our second row forwards on that tour, who had played in France, for the Brive club, for four seasons and spoke French like the locals. Fitzie knew the history, the culture and the background of the people and the area like that vast, squashed, battered area which is the back of his own hand. He took us to a couple of places, telling us all about the region and what had happened there in history, especially during the years of the German occupation from 1940 to 1944. It was fascinating; I would say I learned more from that single experience than weeks studying a textbook could have taught me.

Would it not be equally beneficial for an Englishman, a Scot, a Welshman or an Irishman to fly out to Australia or New Zealand and spend a few months there, perhaps as a guest of the local club, playing his rugby for them and learning about another lifestyle on the other side of the world? How many players, those who might not be involved in international rugby tours but are still pretty useful performers on the field, would get such an opportunity? This seems to me an area where rugby can make such a valuable contribution to life in general. You should always be able to say you have learned a lot from any overseas tour. No matter if training, preparation and the actual playing of games make a sightseeing trip every day of the tour impossible, you can still say truthfully that you have learned all manner of things about the country you have visited.

You will gather from all of this that I see no harm, no danger to either the individual or the game in this movement of players between hemispheres. Ah, I can hear the authorities saying, but what about the physical commitment required, the toll such sustained first-class rugby would take on a player's body? Players have to be protected from themselves, the authorities reason – when it suits them. But when there is the question of an overseas tour and, naturally, they want their best players to be involved, then such concern seems mysteriously to take a back seat. Which is all very curious.

I am firmly of the opinion that grown men, many of them in responsible jobs as doctors, solicitors, law students and so forth are perfectly capable of making a simple decision about whether their bodies need a rest. I honestly do not think that the authorities need to lay down laws to prevent these people from playing themselves into the gutter of injury because they are incapable of deciding their own fate. On one hand you have the authorities praising the players in their sport as mature, impeccable young men (the majority of them, anyway) and on the other, the situation whereby those in charge seem to want to treat the players like schoolboys. They cannot have it both ways.

England is one of the countries that has voiced opposition to the idea of players switching hemispheres to continue playing rugby in their own off-season. Yet, after as intense a winter season as England had in 1989-90, in which they missed a Grand Slam by only a few points in their only defeat against Scotland, the English Rugby Union fixed up a summer tour of Argentina, in July and August of all times, during which they were to play two Test matches against the Pumas. That is having your cake and eating it in my language.

Few countries can escape censure on this point. When Alan Jones, the former Australian coach, talked about the players being used as mobile bank accounts to fuel the coffers of the game, he hit the nail right on the head. Australia have done it when it has suited them; so have New Zealand, I am sure. So have most countries in the world, because the players are always expendable. So what if David Campese wrecks his knee and cannot play for the Wallabies any more? Who would really care, apart from yours truly? Would the authorities in Britain have wrung their hands in despair had I, or Nick Farr-Jones, or Michael Lynagh, gone down with a shocking injury just weeks before the 1991 World Cup which prevented us from playing in that tournament? They might have expressed some genuine measure of sympathy but that would have been as far as it would have extended. And the reason is that the tournament was guaranteed to make an extraordinary sum of money months, and maybe a couple of years, before it even started.

What was really essential to the authorities was to arrange and preside over an event which grossed a really significant amount of cash. Whether Nick Farr-Jones captained Australia or David Campese missed the tournament was not an urgent priority on their list. So when such people say that players should not be allowed to move from different hemispheres to continue playing rugby it rings a bit hollow as far as I am concerned. Year-round rugby has been known before, and from what I understand, it has been welcomed by those involved. The London club Blackheath recruited the then Randwick scrum-half and captain Brad Burke, later to become a Wallaby and later still to turn professional with Eastern Surburbs in Sydney, for a season in English rugby. Brad certainly learned a lot from the experience and he made some good friends from his time in London. He also came back to Randwick with some great stories about Welsh referees from when Blackheath had played clubs like Neath down in South Wales. Blackheath got something out of it because Brad's experience helped the other guys there, and he enjoyed a few months living in England and seeing another aspect of the game.

I imagine Northampton felt the same way about the help the former All Black captain Wayne Shelford must have given them during his time with the English midlands club in the 1990-91 winter in the UK. Would playing through the winter in England following a season with North Harbour back home in New Zealand have damaged, in any sense, Buck Shelford's powerful body? I very much doubt it. Buck would probably clobber you if you even made the suggestion to him personally! The Irish international second row forward Noel Francis played a few games in Australia for Manly after the 1987 World Cup, and big Noel always reckoned he learned a heck of a lot about the game in his short stay. He had a good time, too, by all accounts, which is just as important.

I can say without the slightest hesitation that I have never suffered physically from my 12-month involvement in the game. Nor do I believe it affects your performance on the field. You just have to learn when to taper off a bit and when to climb back hard into the physical fitness required to handle Test match rugby. It must be said that living and working in Italy is a pleasure, and I am always happy to go back there at the start of the winter season. In 1990, for example, I was on an early plane out of London's Heathrow Airport the morning after the final match of the Barbarians Centenary celebration week, against Wales at Cardiff. At 5.00 am I dashed in a taxi from our Cardiff hotel to the airport. True, it was partly because I wanted to see the World Cup qualifying match between Italy and Romania that day in Padua, but it was still a great feeling to get back to Italy and meet up once again with all my old friends.

Years ago, of course, rugby players who played the whole year round were as rare a species as Italians who didn't like soccer! This was because most players had specialised careers and were able to fit the game into their schedules only through the willingness of their bosses to be generous with time off, and because of their own determination to combine business and sport for a few years. In my case, I enjoy the game so much that rugby *is* my career. I believe that if you do the right things through rugby, you can survive from the game by doing public relations work, maybe even some modelling of clothes or speaking at public events, perhaps on behalf of a company. I was asked to do PR work for Taronga Zoo in Sydney a couple of years ago and I enjoyed it immensely. The authorities there clearly wanted to use my name because I was known in Sydney, and I was able to help them in a variety of ways. I helped with the corporate sponsorship of certain enclosures and raised around $130,000 in three or four months. Without rugby, would the name of David Campese have meant anything to the zoo authorities in Sydney in their efforts to attract more financial support? Of course not. This is what I mean by surviving from the game. I have also worked for other companies in Australia and I have now acquired a fair amount of experience in the way the world of public relations gets along. I hope that experience will see me right when I finally finish playing rugby.

Rugby already demands much greater standards of fitness and preparation than it used to. It has come a long way since the beginning of the 1980s when I started to play. These days, it is a much faster game; there are many more Test matches, so players at the top level have to be 120 per cent fit rather than just 100 per cent. It has become rather like an athlete's preparation for the Olympic Games, where he gives up his work to concentrate for four years on the event. Four years' devotion to a single race, or perhaps a single match – how many people ever envisage that happening in Rugby Union? But far from being a dot on the horizon, it is already virtually a reality in a great many countries.

In Australia, we start training for the new season in December, around the time when everyone else is drinking and eating to celebrate Christmas. From that time onwards, our bodies have to be as finely tuned as a high performance motor car. They must be in peak condition at pre-arranged times – match day in other words – while the rest of the week they are kept idling, ready for that explosion of action. Our season does not even start until April, or at least it used not to, but suddenly, in recent years, the top players have been confronted with a major tournament right at the start of the season. The South Pacific Championship was an idea conceived by the game's authorities in the southern hemisphere (who else) to promote interest and raise more funds (of course). It contains the best provincial sides from Australia and New Zealand as well as the Fijian national team. The intensity of it is frightening. It is like playing five Test matches within the space of a month. You could be meeting the New Zealand champions Auckland one week, flying across the Tasman Sea to play them at Eden Park, and then returning home to meet the physically tough Fijians in Sydney just a week later. Then you might head up to Brisbane to play Queensland or entertain Wellington or Canterbury, neither of whom are exactly lightweights in the world game, to complete your involvement in the tournament. And all this before you have kicked a ball in international rugby that season. Years ago, pre-season training did not start until February at the earliest. But if you want to be in the sort of top physical shape the modern game demands, then today you need to be hard at work a great deal earlier than that.

So now you are into your domestic season. You might play as many as five or six Test matches during that season, as well as facing Queensland a couple of times in highly competitive state games. And after all that, you could be off to New Zealand for a six-week tour comprising as many as 12 matches which represent the absolute peak, in terms of physical effort and high-class skill, of what you are likely to encounter anywhere in the world. Believe me, if you go to New Zealand anything short of maximum fitness, you will be found out in the first match.

When the Wallabies are touring the UK, they do not leave Australia until late September or early October. By then, the club season has reached its climax and you can bet that Randwick will have been involved in the final. This is another supreme test of body and skill but, not content with that exhausting run-in to the end of the season, the authorities recently instigated another match – the top Queensland club side against the New South Wales champions. If ever a match was unwanted and unloved by the players and merely a brutal, naked attempt to extract still more money from them in the domestic season, then this is surely it. You complete that match at the end of September and then go straight into training camp with the Wallabies for their UK tour. This summary of a leading player's typical schedule has not, of course, even mentioned the weekend training camps with the Wallabies when you are away with the squad, perhaps from Friday evening to late on Sunday. And such commitments are becoming increasingly frequent.

A few years ago, I sat down at home in Sydney and thought long and hard about all this commitment to the game. I felt that if I was going to spend so much time training and working out to keep myself in top condition, it would be best if I could sustain that by playing on through the greater part of the year. You don't really get stale from playing rugby, just sick of training. And constant training without a match at the end of the week is the hardest. I could play rugby five days a week, but training is like going to work, sitting down and writing reports. You have to do it day after day and therefore it becomes a great deal more monotonous than playing.

Training on your own is the hardest of all. When you train alone, it is desperately difficult to build yourself to a peak because you have no points of comparison. You think you are doing well, but then you start training with a team again and invariably find that you are not as fit either as you should be or as you thought you were. To train by yourself, you need a lot of dedication and drive and you must have a long-term goal to strive for. You become very used to driving yourself to targets because no one else is going to do it. That is why I train so much, every day in fact.

Yet if I were to give up rugby tomorrow, my involvement in the game has been so heavy in recent years that I honestly feel I would even miss the training. I would be like a junkie denied his daily fix! I cannot envisage ever giving up training totally for two reasons. First, despite the loneliness and difficulties, I enjoy the feeling of physical fitness. I do not drink very much at all and never smoke. I hate it when people smoke near me. It is a shocking habit which is positively harmful to your health. Secondly, I have seen too many sportsmen let their bodies go to waste once they have retired. Maintaining a fitness schedule once you have hung up your boots must require immense discipline, but I intend to do this when I finish. I will still play golf and some other sports after rugby, so fitness would remain among my priorities. Physical fitness brings a mental alertness; you feel good in yourself. You sense a sharpness which is missing when you are out of condition.

My former Australian team-mate, Mark Ella, ballooned from 80 kilos to 90 after he retired. The guy looked like a fat little roly-poly! It is sad to see a player like him put on all that weight, it just does not look right. Mark, I am happy to say, has since trimmed that little barrel shape into a reasonable figure. He gave up his job in Sydney and came out to Italy to play a final season of rugby with me in 1990. After regaining his fitness he became coach to my Italian club, Amatori of Milan. I hope he stays in shape because it has to be dangerous to anyone's health to put on that kind of weight. Businessmen do not keel over from heart attacks for no good reason; the lives they lead and the amount of food and drink they consume are invariably major factors in their illness.

When I am not playing rugby or training, golf is my other main passion – I play off a handicap of 8. I also like tennis, squash and swimming, any sport, really, with an element of physical fitness. I will have a go at anything, and in Australia you can do just that because the climate is so conducive to outdoor sporting activity. I have not had a summer off in Australia for the last few years, but that does not concern me. I know that if I were to have three months away from rugby, perhaps sitting around on the beach and having a good time, it would be incredibly hard to start up again afterwards. In my 12-month training schedule I take short breaks and don't train as hard sometimes, but when I want a higher level of physical condition I can step it up quite quickly.

Undoubtedly, sprint work is the hardest training exercise. It is tough, relentless and a physical strain. There is no real pleasure in it; you just do it because you need to raise that side of your game to be in top shape.

Wherever I am in the world, I check out the local facilities. If I am on tour with the Wallabies, good facilities are usually laid on for us. On the 1988 Wallaby tour in Britain, for instance, after our squad training each morning I would spend most afternoons in a nearby gymnasium, pounding weights and doing stretch exercises and sit-ups to tone my body for the demands to be made on it. This was one of the reasons why I performed so well on that tour. Another was my desire to show that my poor performances towards the end of Alan Jones' time as Wallaby coach were partly due to a lack of confidence brought about by his criticisms of me. Deep down, I wanted to prove that I still had it and could be a great player.

Rugby has now become an entirely different game, notably in the last few years. Even players well away from the forward exchanges, such as wings and full-backs, need physical power in their upper body to release the ball in the tackle or to hold an opponent and try to seize possession. In the past, wings used to run down the touchline and full-backs just kicked the ball into touch. But it's very different today, and if you are not in the best physical condition you fail at the highest level.

I try to work out in a gymnasium, doing a good 60 minutes in each session, at least three times a week. Then there is sprint work, simple running and also training with my club or national team. All this takes a great deal of time and energy. For example, when you do sprint training, you cannot just get out there and do a couple of laps and then call it a day. You must prepare, change, warm up thoroughly and then start work for a lengthy period of time. Afterwards, you wind down, change, shower and go back to your hotel or wherever you happen to be living. All this makes for a pretty lonely existence. I have had one fiancée and one particular Italian girlfriend with whom I was very close. My fiancée, Cindy, and I spent five happy years together. We suited each other well and had a great time. I learned a lot from her, for she understood rugby and made some very helpful suggestions which I adopted. But it petered out in time and that was a pity. In Italy, I had a lovely relationship with Monica, but that came to an end too, quite recently. I am used to being by myself because of my way of life in the last five years. I have spent some months here, some there, perhaps a few more in another place in another year and so on, and it is all desperately hard if you are trying to have a relationship with someone. A girlfriend cannot necessarily just throw up her work and fly around the world to be with a player. And what if she did? How fair would it be to fly someone across the world and then go out training for three or four hours every day? She would probably hardly see her partner and be bored to death.

To the outsider, I suppose my lifestyle looks attractive, perhaps even glamorous. Some people have told me what a lovely easy life I lead, but my answer is that it might also be pretty easy for me to go round the bend. But sometimes I look at others who think they have mundane lives and feel that it would be nice to be in their position. Some regular work, a family and more of a settled life. It would not be me, though. I concede that there are many things I *want* to do by myself. I think the South African player, Naas Botha, who also plays in Italy in the northern hemisphere season, is a bit like me. In a relationship, it can be hard to explain to somebody: 'Look, I just want to be by myself'. And it is especially difficult if children are involved. Indeed, there is probably no point in having children if you do not spend as much time as possible with them. So, for the moment at least, I am happy enough to be alone. I will drive to visit places or go shopping alone. I like cooking, so looking after myself is not such a great hardship; indeed, I quite like it at times. I enjoy my own company.

Of course, when you are on tour with 30 guys, it is great. But I know it is only for a short time so I prepare myself to switch back to the solitary life I have chosen. Having Mark Ella around in Milan for the last two winters has been great for me, but I don't spend every minute in Mark's pocket. He has his wife Kim and little daughter Nicole with him, and occasionally I share a meal with them. More often than not, though, I return to my flat after training and cook something. They say all Italians love to get their hands on a frying pan so perhaps some of the old blood from my Italian ancestry points me towards the cooker! I have always had a good time in Italy whether I have been mainly on my own or with someone. It is a part of my life I will always remember with a great deal of affection.

As for rugby, and that film producer's theory that I was the trail-blazer for a future trend (that film was never made in the end!), I doubt whether this lifestyle, wrapped up in the game, will become universal. As I have intimated, the authorities seem against the idea of players switching hemispheres. When I first went to Italy all you needed was the permission of your club and the ARU. Now, six years later, you have to fill in four or five different forms asking what you do, whether you receive money from work and what kind of toothpaste you use. It's a damned impertinence in a game which is supposed to be all about freedom and personal choice. The authorities are cracking down, making it harder for you to go where you want and do what you want. More obviously, some players simply would not *want* to play the game for 12 months. It is already difficult enough for some players to devote the time they do to rugby. I can't see someone like Nick Farr-Jones giving up his legal work to concentrate totally on rugby – his job is his career. In Australia, we have always had guys retiring young from the game because their work was more important to them. I see that state of affairs continuing into the future for a great many players, despite the tinkering with the laws on amateurism which took place at the International Rugby Board's meeting in Edinburgh in late 1990.

Few Australians will make much out of the game in terms of sideline activities for the simple reason that the authorities may not allow us to capitalise on the promotion of products directly associated with the game. Besides, Rugby Union in our country is just not big enough. Rugby League, yes, but not Union. In Australia, there are so many sports that Rugby Union comes well down the list. And it is really only in a country where the game is the chief interest or one of the top sports, such as New Zealand, that players might make some reasonable money. In Australia, players will continue to be lost to Rugby League because it is *the* sport of our land. If the amateur rules emerge as workable and fair to the players, then I would hope to make some capital from my association with the game. I would hope, for example, that some leading company in Australia, whatever their field, might wish to have a 'name' from the world of sport to represent them, speak to their young executives, perhaps, or to attend official functions to promote the company's name and image. But I still have my doubts because, as I say, Rugby League is the king in our country and it is a fact of life that Wally Lewis is an altogether bigger fish than David Campese.

So in response to the suggestion that I have set a trend, my answer is that I do not believe others will necessarily follow. Only certain players will ever do it; indeed, only a few would ever *want* to. Just ask many of the world's top players and you will find that the idea of playing 12 months each year is about as attractive to them as being trapped at the bottom of a ruck with the boots piling in! And I can understand that, for it is a totally different, at times almost alien existence, which certainly would not suit everyone. Personally speaking, I will continue to do it for as long as it does not affect my performances in top-grade rugby. I readily concede that playing in Italy does affect your sharpness for the basic reason that you do a lot of things there which you would never do in Australian club rugby, let alone international rugby. The best analogy I can draw is to say that if you always drove your car on a private road and never had to bother about giving signals or observing the laws of the road, then it would be poor preparation for returning to the busy main streets of a city. It can be done – but I need a short period to readapt back in Australia before my game acclimatises to the superior level of the game at home.

In 1989 I made a mistake. I went straight home at the end of the Italian season and immediately played representative football, which was simply not possible. I found myself making elementary errors which should never be a part of the better player's game. But I learned my lesson from that, and now I try to ensure that I have time to adapt to the higher demands in Australia.

In my rugby life I must have no distractions. I must play rugby and concentrate 100 per cent on it, play and train hard. Other players could perhaps do things differently but this method suits me best. It is the core of my approach to life and sport and it explains why I am prepared to be alone. I seek a level of commitment to the game which is, by its very nature, selfish in the context of a relationship. I have never felt able to combine the two with anything approaching satisfaction. One or the other invariably suffers, and as I am devoted to the sport which is my life, relationships do not endure. For instance, I usually see my family only two or three times a year. In 1990, I saw my parents just three times in the four months I spent in Australia because of my work as a sales executive with the Pepsi-7-Up company and my commitments to rugby. That has so far been the harsh reality, but I hope one day the situation may be different.

CHAPTER
— 3 —

ITALY

I cried tears of loneliness and trepidation on my first night alone in Italy. Today, seven years later, I can never wait to get back to the country. Perhaps those conflicting emotions typify Italy and the Italians, for the country and her people are high-spirited, friendly, emotional and perhaps a shade unpredictable. As I have Italian blood in my veins (don't ask me what the percentage is!), maybe I have those qualities too.

My memories of my early life in the country are sketchy, as they are bound to be considering that I was so young. My father came from a little village named Montecchio Pre, north-west of Padua, in the north of Italy. I lived there for about three years, from the age of two. I was born in Australia, but Dad wanted to return home to see his family. He had gone out to Australia in the early 1950s: times were hard in Italy after the war, and the economy was not strong. Montecchio was just a small village in a poor area and the lure of a new country, with all the opportunities it was said emigrants would find there, proved attractive. Other people from the area went to countries like Argentina and the United States of America.

When we went back to Dad's village, we were there for a lot longer than just a holiday so I had to go to the local school. What I learned, or how I learned it, remembering that I was only just beginning to get to grips with some of the basic rudiments of English, I am not quite sure! But I still managed to make a name for myself fairly quickly in the local neighbourhood.

My Dad's parents lived opposite a farm, just beside a little country road: one of those delightful tracks which seem to wind their way all over the lovely countryside of nothern Italy once you leave the big conurbations like Milan. One day, when I was about three or four years old, I walked over the road to the farm, quite unannounced, and climbed up on to a large tractor. You could blame some poor farm worker for leaving the means in place to start this wretched machine but I think the idiot who actually turned the key, yours truly, would have to take the major share of the blame. Well, the inevitable happened. The tractor started up and I drove it . . . straight into a wall! Crash. Badly buckled tractor, badly dented wall. Badly bashed boy, too, for although I wasn't hurt by the collision, I remember suffering by Dad's hand a few minutes later! Of course, the moment it happened, I knew the trouble I would be in, and sure enough I got a belting when I got home.

It's funny, but no matter how old you are you tend to remember incidents such as that. I was used to climbing up into machines because there was nothing I liked more than sitting up in a big pick-up truck alongside my father when he went to work on the farm. I would ride alongside him through the Italian fields, shimmering in the summer heat, and be quite oblivious of the dust and dirt. My Dad could shift anything: building materials, farm machinery, anything.

I enjoyed my time in Italy as a young boy. Had my father said we were staying there forever, I would not have minded at all. I could not remember much about Australia and it was impossible to understand how far away the place was. Had I stayed, I guess I would not have become a rugby player. Inevitably, soccer would have been the focus of my attention had I been any good at it. Who knows, today I might have been playing for Internazionale, the big Milan club, or Juventus of Turin. *'Viva Campo!'*, they might have been screaming at the Stadio Comunale or the San Siro. And the young millionaire out in the middle might just have raised an arm, in the style of a Roman Emperor, to acknowledge the adulation of 90,000 fans. Ah well, back to the world of reality.

When I went back to Italy in 1984 after the Australian Wallabies' Grand Slam tour of Britain and Ireland, I went back to the small village where my grandparents lived. And I remembered at once the small road and the brick wall I had demolished. I was pleased to see that it had been rebuilt by then, and that apparently no other local lad had driven a tractor into it!

The opportunity to play in Italy came comparatively early on in my international career, just two years after I had made my international debut for Australia. We were about to embark upon the 1984 tour to Great Britain and Ireland, my third major overseas tour (I had been to Italy a year earlier as part of the trip to France with the Wallabies), when Roger Gould, the big Queensland full-back who was to play such a crucial role in the success of that tour, called me at home in Queanbeyan. He had an unusual offer to make me. 'How do you fancy staying over in Italy after the tour finishes in December, spending Christmas there and playing for a club until the end of the Italian season in May?' he enquired. 'Tell me more', I said. Roger had been talking to a club in northern Italy named Petrarca. I thought about the strange new world I would be entering. I wanted to take up the challenge, see how I would fare, how I could do alone. It would be my first stay away from Australia for any period of time, and I wanted to see how I would cope. The reality shocked me.

What happened on tour before that, is sufficiently documented elsewhere. But I have to say that the fact that the 1984 Wallabies became so close made my subsequent lifestyle all the harder. We blazed a glorious trail through Great Britain: we overcame a hopeless first half against England at Twickenham to win in a canter and we thrashed Wales at Cardiff. We negotiated Ireland's exceptional hospitality and didn't feel bad at all in saying a special thank you by handing them a thumping defeat at Lansdowne Road. We stuck together like glue; we became mates and the closer we grew the more successful we became. Australian rugby had never known such highs, but what goes up must come down, and I half-sensed that a crash was coming for me.

Someone once told me the story of a British journalist who covered a tour lasting almost five months in Australia and New Zealand in 1966. On the final night he sat at the bar, alone, wishing it could all go on forever, while most of his homesick colleagues could hardly wait for the plane to depart on the first leg home. Maybe some of us on that 1984 Wallaby tour felt similarly, but we knew another world, another life and a different time lay ahead of us. Mark Ella would be gone before our next major overseas challenge, the 1986 tour to New Zealand, and some other famous faces would also be missing. Life would move on.

It moved on for me, too. Roger and I flew to Italy as soon as the tour ended at Cardiff against the Barbarians, the final leg of the Grand Slam having been completed against Scotland at Murrayfield, and I found myself catapulted into a strange new world. It was as though the dark clouds forewarning the isolation I would feel started to build up as soon as we took off from London's Heathrow Airport. An hour and a half later, we arrived in Italy, a country where hardly anyone had ever heard of the Wallabies or David Campese. Suddenly, all our glories, our triumphs and our shared delights seemed in the very distant past. None of that counted any more.

We found ourselves in a place somewhere quite close to the town of Padua. I was in my room when the telephone rang and a voice told me there were some people to see me waiting downstairs. I could not work this out; who did I know in this part of Italy? Perhaps it was just the old story: someone wanted a ticket and they had chosen my name at random from the pile to introduce themselves. Still, I went downstairs, and what an extraordinary sight greeted me. Roger Gould, who spoke good Italian from his time playing club rugby in the country, was with me, and what a good investment he proved to be! No sooner had we descended the stairs than about 30 Italians clustered around me, talking nineteen to the dozen, and slapping me firmly on the back, all at the same time, or so it seemed. I realised at once who they were – my relatives from northern Italy. They had commandeered cars, bikes and vans to get to the hotel where we were staying to welcome me. And what a wonderful welcome it was!

They greeted me, they hugged me – was this what it felt like to win a World Cup soccer tournament for Italy? Adulation had arrived. The only problem was, I didn't have a clue what any of them were saying. And were they talking – words were flowing like wine on a good Italian evening. It didn't seem to matter in the least that I could not reply; they just went on talking to me, and if I didn't reply, they just started on at someone else. I kept lurching towards Roger, saying 'Hey, mate, what is this one saying?' and 'What does that one mean exactly?', when hand signals and willing signs were simply not enough to break the language barrier. They finally decided that a true Italian welcome had been given, and retired for the night. And so did we, bruised and battered from all the back-slapping and hearty greetings. 'Gee', said Roger, at some stage later that night, 'are you going to have a great time here!'

And he was right, of course. But first, there was the considerable hurdle of homesickness to negotiate. And it proved as intimidating a barrier as Becher's Brook, that huge fence they put up on the English Grand National course at Aintree. The day Roger left, there I was, a little boy aged 23 in a strange new country where I didn't speak a word of the language. I didn't know what I was doing. I was the only foreign player at the club and I found it a weird experience, especially after being away on tour with 30 blokes. Had my knowledge of geography and the world been somewhat more enhanced, I might have been aware of what a fabulous area I was in. Padua is not that far from Venice, one of the jewels in the European crown. You could ask a thousand young guys in Australia today if they fancied the idea of going to stay in accommodation which was provided for them, with the job of playing rugby, all for nothing, basically, and I'm willing to bet that 999 of them would grab the chance! I would, too – today. But in 1984, I looked at things a bit differently. And that first night in Padua, I went back to my accommodation alone, lay on my bed and couldn't stop the tears of homesickness. I felt just the same as countless other 23-year-olds when they have found themselves alone on the other side of the world. OK, maybe that shatters the illusion of the much-travelled world sportsman, but we are all the same deep down: I just wanted to catch the first plane home, whenever it was leaving, from whichever airport. That was all.

But, of course, morning comes, and with it a whole new perspective and a re-evaluation. One man arrived at my flat that morning, and I can say without exaggeration that he made *the* difference between me flying home and staying – for six years of Italian rugby seasons, and six years of delight. Vittorio Munari might not have looked like a knight in shining armour but he seemed that way to me! Vittorio and his wife Daniela looked after me superbly; they took me under their wing and I was allowed to adapt slowly, and often in the sanctuary of their home, to life in a different country. Anyone who has travelled overseas, even guys who have been doing it for 20 years, prefers staying with a friend or in a private home, where there is some conversation, some normal life. Hotels are impersonal places, the same the world over. You enter as a total stranger and depart in the same category. There is no chance to sit down, shake off your boots and have a good, homely chat with someone; it's all strictly formal outside the confines of your private, sealed, isolated room. Inside, there is an almost antiseptic atmosphere; beyond, the rush and bustle of total strangers passing, like ships in the night.

Vittorio spoke excellent English, which, for me, was like finding shelter on a windswept night, and everything was made a lot easier because of him and Daniela. They showed me enormous kindness for which I shall forever be grateful. Vittorio is now on the Italian Federation, and you could not find a better man to represent rugby.

Things were clearly very new to me when I arrived in Padua. I certainly got a shock when I turned up for my first training session: I put on some old, half-dirty kit to wear for training – you never look very smart in your training gear. But waiting to greet me that day was a very special welcoming party, thousands of them! As I ran out on to the training ground, I heard the collective cheer of many voices behind me. Mystified, I looked up to see the whole grandstand filled! They had come, so I was told, just to see me train. Italy must be the only rugby-playing country of the world where that happens. What would the crusty colonels and majestic majors down at Twickenham have said?

It quickly became apparent that I needed to make some sort of impact fairly soon with Petrarca. People would surely not take all this trouble to come and watch a fool – I had to perform and do a few things well if I was to be accepted. Yet I could neither converse with, nor share the real, in-depth ideas of my team-mates even though some of them spoke a smattering of English – some dilemma! Again, Vittorio came to the rescue. He was good with the team, knew a lot about rugby and willingly helped me integrate. Without him, I wonder whether I would have stayed, and had I not I would have missed out on what has been a wonderful interlude in my rugby-playing life. He made my job so much easier and the players responded, too, I'm sure because of Vittorio's urgings. Complete strangers came up to me and tried to help, offering whatever assistance was appropriate. I am sure Vittorio instigated all of this. That would be typical of him.

I stayed with Petrarca three years. In that time, we won two premierships, great achievements in Italian rugby. And very well fêted we were too. There were some big matches in those days. I remember one year, 1985 I think it was, playing against a Treviso team which included the New Zealand All Black John Kirwan. A crowd of around 10,000 crammed in to see that home match. It might have been exceptional in terms of our average gate, which was nearer 4,000, but even this was higher than in many areas of Italian rugby. In the north of Italy interest in rugby is strong because the area is unaffected to a large extent by the soccer clubs. No major Italian First Division teams are based here: Milan would be the nearest, and that is two hours away. In the north, there are Treviso, Petrarca and Rovigo, names which are synonymous with great Italian rugby. Here, men of world renown such as the late, great Welshman Carwyn James, and the Frenchman, Pierre Villepreux, have coached, coaches who excited the players, men who made you wish you could have got out on to the training ground with them to share in their deep knowledge of the game and their love for the finer values of the sport.

The Petrarca club lent me a little flat in the centre of the town, functional and friendly, once I realised that there were familiar faces around, people who would be happy to see me and with whom I could share some time. It was an ordinary one-bedroomed affair, but I wasn't going to argue. I have never needed a king's palace to stay in and I have always been happy with what I have been given. I know some people think you would want a vast, luxury apartment but that's not my style. After all, I was comparatively new on the international scene and residing in a new country. Besides, I am not the kind of person who demands something better all the time. I would not have dreamed of saying 'Look, I want something bigger and better'. Whatever else I might be accused of, I don't think greed is a failing of mine.

Anyway, once I had settled down and accepted life in another country, the challenge side of the equation took over. I fancied the idea of looking after myself and getting through my early difficulties. You learn a lot about yourself and your character in that kind of situation. If you can handle looking after yourself and adapting to your own company, then I think you can feel you have passed a test, negotiated a mental barrier. This was the first time I had looked after myself away from Australia or anywhere, in fact. I had shipped out of home once before, then I went back again – Mother's cooking is always best! Six months by yourself in an unfamiliar country – you cannot find a tougher introduction to travel than that. And once I sat down to think about it, I began to relish the challenge.

During those six months I was to know terrible loneliness at times, even acknowledging the great friendship of people like Vittorio and Giacomo, another close friend. I came to call them Pixie and Dixie, because they were both small, around 5 feet 4 inches. Both liked having a good time and playing jokes and remain great friends. I could not speak the language then so did not understand the television. That was a major disadvantage. However, I stayed, survived and came to enjoy my time there, principally because of the people with whom I came into contact. Some of the players who understood a little English would take me out with them sometimes, which was kind. Italians are really into families and I was welcomed like I was one of their own. I appreciated it at the time and have been extremely grateful ever since. It was quickly apparent that if you treated them nicely, they would do the same in return. Treat them poorly, act the big star, and you could forget any welcome; which was fair enough.

I think the fact that I have always been an ordinary bloke helped me. I have never tried to go anywhere showing off or saying stupid things like 'Don't you know who I am?', the classic phrase some people in the limelight seem to trot out, as though it should automatically lead everyone to bow down before them. I hate that kind of person and I have never understood that attitude; it is arrogant and unbelievably short-sighted. People loathe you for that, and why shouldn't they? In Padua, I just walked around in an ordinary track-suit. I wasn't worried about looking the part and I was perfectly happy to greet people if they wanted to talk. Civility costs nothing might be an old saying, but it is as true today as it ever was. I signed autographs if anyone wanted them, as I still do today. What is a moment of my time if a child wants my autograph? I do demand one thing from them, though – courtesy in asking. I like people to say please. If they cannot do that, I wonder why I should take the time to sign for them. Civility works both ways.

By the time I had spent three years in Padua, people had got to know me quite well and I had made some good friends. Rugby was pretty big in the town so our sport enjoyed high profile. We were winning most of the time, too, and that helped fuel interest. You can take two attitudes when you find yourself in that situation. The first is to take the rugby seriously, train as hard as you can and generally regard the whole exercise as one in which you should excel as often as possible. The second is to regard it as a paid holiday in which you have to play a bit of rugby from time to time as your part of the bargain, not treating it too seriously because you are basically there to see the country and have a good time. I adhered firmly to the former attitude. I always took it seriously and would never go out the night before a game. I trained hard, stayed in good shape physically and tried to help the others if they wanted assistance. I always tried hard in every match, and I like to think they respected me for that. I heard of one Italian club which signed up another Australian player who was often to be seen out in bars, cafés or clubs until around three o'clock on the morning of a match. He ate well, drank a fair amount and had a rattling good time, but when the team lost, he would get the blame. I never did those things, not because I am some pariah of virtue but because it would have meant abusing people's commitment, hospitality and desire to see their team win. Oh, and because it would have been completely unprofessional.

I suppose that guy took the view that the rugby was pretty ordinary at times compared to what he was used to and that he could just float through matches and still turn in a reasonable performance, all of which was probably quite true. But you would never catch me adopting that attitude because I like winning too much. I don't care whether it is a Grand Final with Randwick, a Wallaby international against New Zealand or an Italian club match – the burning desire to win never leaves me. That desire sustains me through the long hours, weeks and months of solitary training when it would be altogether easier to quit. I could kid myself I was fit enough and that would probably be true. I could bow to the voice which tells you that you're in good enough shape, so why push on? I push on because I want to be that extra percentage fit, because it could mean the narrow difference between winning and losing. In Italy, it mattered to me that we won, but then it does wherever in the world I play. The fact that this was Italian rugby in no way diminished my thirst for victory each time I went out on to the field. To me, winning is everything and transmitting that attitude to the other players is undoubtedly part of my job when I am in Italy.

I do not believe I am there to be judged on whether I play well or badly. I see my role as helping the players to understand better how to play the game, how to become better performers and how to lift their skills. I know how I can play and people generally know what I can and cannot do. In Italy, the overseas player is expected to play all the time at his best, and if he cannot do that in return for what they are doing for him, then they do not like it. And I don't think you can blame them. If you are invited over to play in a foreign country, you live nicely and enjoy a good standard of living. It is a marvellous opportunity to go abroad and play rugby while earning a living from some promotional work for the club or its sponsors. Rugby has given me a lot: education; seeing the world and how people live in it; the opportunity to meet and talk to different people and make friends. You can widen your knowledge of the world, and for me that has been an invaluable experience because I was never very bright at school. History or subjects like that never interested me much, but I have had the perfect opportunity to broaden my mind. I have enjoyed my time in Italy immensely. It is a beautiful country, there is so much to see and the people, as I have said, are delightful. The food suits me, too, as someone who wants to look after his body: I eat lots of pasta and, of course, there is no better place in the world for that. I rarely eat red meat or drink alcohol, so Italian cuisine is ideal. I think it has been proven as an extremely healthy, balanced diet.

I am strongly into educating people in what they eat, but as regards education on a wider scale, I would say that my biggest problem in life was that at school, I was not interested in studies, only sport. I loved every minute of sport, whatever we were playing; the time when we put away our schoolbooks and went out to play sport was the best. I finally left school a year before I was supposed to because I had no interest in it. With hindsight and maturity, I am able to see that that was wrong. Going to Italy, which is so rich in architecture, history and culture, makes me wish I had learned more at school. So my advice now to anybody about playing rugby, or indeed any sport, would be to finish their studies first. Never take short cuts, which is what I did: studies are too important to throw away.

Living in a country is so much better than touring. These days, tours seem so rushed that you have little time to meet people and have a decent look at the country you're visiting. In this respect, the attitude of governing bodies in the game disappoints me. If you finish a tour of France in Paris, for example, why can they not arrange an extra couple of days so that the players can see the sights and enjoy themselves before flying home? The French themselves did that after the 1986 World Cup and again after their 1990 tour to Australia. Both times, they spent a few days resting up and having a look at islands in the Pacific (although on the second trip tragedy struck during the short break en route for home when front row forward Dominique Bouet died in his hotel room). I do think that the current trend of teams just finishing their last match, having a meal and then getting straight on the plane for home the very next day ought to be revised.

I mentioned the good lifestyle a rugby player can enjoy in Italy and I'd like to expand that. I do not deny, for example, that I have got something financially out of going to Italy – how else could I have lived there? But it has been done through promotional work, which I am entitled to do because I have no other occupation. I work sometimes for a travel agency, Five Viaggio, which is a company associated with Silvio Berlusconi. I have an allowance as well as expenses. My contract with the Italian club includes the provision of some PR work: I go along to a store if there is a promotion and wear the gear. That is my job besides playing rugby. So whenever the club wants to promote the game in Milan, they use me as part of their programme, and this is arranged by the club and the Italian Federation for the club's main sponsors. This has provided me with a good income, rather, I imagine, as the legitimate business activities of the England captain, Will Carling, help him to earn a living. It might be different from, say, doing an orthodox job as a bank manager or an accountant, but it is within the laws as I have read them these past years if you have no other source of income.

The Italians have seen no reason to hide such matters and I find that refreshing. There was talk that they were even paying their international squad players a basic fee of around $30,000 (£12,000) to be available for squad sessions and training throughout the season. With that level of commitment on the part of the authorities, one hopes that the game will really develop in Italy.

The trouble is that the Italian players have not grown up with the game, as they have with soccer. Consequently, they do not really understand rugby and do not have a natural feel for it. This is unfortunate, as is their reluctance to learn about it from others. What you tell a great many of them goes in one ear and out of the other, and I admit it can be difficult telling a 31-year-old prop forward that he is doing it all wrong! Yet to the Italians winning is everything (perhaps that is where my own fanaticism about winning comes from), and so they do want to make strides.

You can be sure of one thing about the Italians and their rugby: as I said before, if you go there just to have a good time and muck about, you won't get invited back. You see, even if the overseas player who is in the nightclub until 3.00 am gets away with it and his team does win. it is not a very clever policy to follow because the other players think they can do the same thing. But they can't. The Italians love to mimic what they see in others. I have been at Italian clubs where the other players have seen me do something and then tried to do exactly the same thing themselves, usually with calamitous results. This is not because I am some sort of superman, but because they have not been practising such special moves, day in day out for years, like I have. But it is the problem: whatever you do they want to copy it. I noticed that even if I ordered an omelette for breakfast on match day, two weeks later the whole team would be ordering omelettes! Once Mark Ella, who was coach to my team Amatori of Milan in 1990, came up to me in the dressing-room before one match and said, 'If I see you strapping one more part of your body I will kill you, because the whole of the team are doing the same and it takes them forever to get ready'! And sure enough, when I glanced across at my team-mates, they were strapping their wrists, knees and anything else I was strapping! They are very easily led, the Italians.

The Campese family continues to thrive in Italy. My father has three brothers, Franco, Mariano and Baltista, and two sisters, Assunta and Silvana, living there with all their families. I was there to see them at Christmas in 1989, and I try to pop up to visit when I can. Because there are so many relatives now, they all fight over where I should go for meals, or where I should stay. One says, 'Come to my place', but another says, 'No, no, he is coming to me'! This can go on for quite some time. Now, when I ring one of them up and say I'm thinking of going to see them, they say to me down the telephone: 'Don't tell anyone else you are coming because they will want you to go to their place'. It is all good natured rivalry, but I find it slightly embarrassing. After all, it's not as if the Pope is coming to tea!

I usually stay with Franco, a lovely, quiet man who would not say boo to a goose. There is no fuss made there, which is the way I like it. I can enjoy a quiet time which suits me best. One year, I had a great honour paid to me when I went to see them all. They took me into the local town, Montecchio, where I was introduced to the local Mayor, who presented me with a plaque of the town, because my father had come from there. I found it slightly strange but very touching. I am a very shy person by nature and I found it extremely difficult when I first went on my own to meet my relatives. I had forgotten most of my Italian and I think the most English any of the relatives spoke was 'hello' and 'goodbye'. I sat there wondering what to do, what to say – all by myself. I decided the way out of this quandary (where was Roger Gould then? Certainly not where he was needed!) was to get stuck into the food. I remember one meal where I ate and ate and ate. And then I ate some more. With a mouthful of food it's easier to look sensible when people talk to you, rather than trying to answer without any real grasp of the language!

Vittorio Munari was also coach of the Petrarca club when I was there and he had a lot of good ideas, particularly about discipline and how to get the players to win. He was a half-back himself, and is one of the keenest students of the game anywhere in the world. He has just about every rugby video ever recorded in a vast library at home and he spends hours just studying the game. He has done that for years. His deep insight into rugby has partly been achieved by watching matches in almost every continent, especially Australia and New Zealand. He knows how to look after the players and he tells them what to do. And they will do it 100 times if need be until they understand what he wants. We won two premierships at Petrarca during my time there. I missed one season in Italy because I went to Sydney to work. Then, in 1987, my last season with the club, we were beaten in the play-offs by Rovigo, the club of Naas Botha. In the 1988 season, I joined Mediolanum Amatori rugby club of Milan.

What a difference I found between the two clubs. At Milan, there was a French coach, Guy Pardies, who wanted to play 15-man rugby with a bunch of players who had no idea about the discipline required to play the running game. Milan is a very wealthy club because it belongs to the Milanese media mogul, Silvio Berlusconi, a man who does not have a problem finding cash to pay the milkman in the morning! But a lot of people hang around the club in Milan, for obvious reasons, and the more games we won, the more people turned up. But when we lost, no one was to be seen! They were a professional club but completely unprofessional, too; they had plenty of money but little idea of the attitude and mentality required to do well on the rugby field. There was no doubt that Milan had a great many good players but they had no idea how to organise them into a good team. And teams win trophies, not individuals.

In the 1989-90 season we even had seven or eight internationals, more than almost any other Italian club, but we still did not win the Italian premiership title because we played too much as individuals when the cohesion of the team most mattered. One reason for that is that all the players have been taught to play the game in different ways. In countries like Australia or England, everyone has a basic idea of rugby; how to tackle, when to pass, when to kick, and so on. But in Italy they do not know any of these things. Even in training, they prefer to have a game because they don't want to spend hours perfecting their skills. They would rather go out and run around bashing each other, trying to win some stupid match. They asked me once to play in one of those games. I said 'Sorry, I am playing on Sunday – I don't want to pick up an injury in a Wednesday training match'. If there is hard work involved, particularly with the improvement of individual skills, they will not do the necessary grafting. In soccer, it is quite different – they will train hard, because that has always been their dream, and anyway, they are probably being made lira billionaires.

The Italian mentality, that great unknown factor, lies behind so many of the problems in their rugby. For a start, that mentality is firmly against change. They do not know how to keep in their minds what they are doing. You might say something to them one night and the very next night they have forgotten all about it. You go there at the start of their season, and six months later you find yourself saying exactly the same things which can be extremely frustrating. I suspect a lot of the guys in rugby just want to see their names in newspapers, fancying the notion of being one of the star men. That has probably come about because the few Italian papers which do cover rugby, squeezing a few lines in between the mass coverage of soccer, tend to mention only the stars. That brings out the worst in the local players!

Mark Ella and I have told our team-mates at Milan time and again that rugby is a 15-man game; it is the strongest *team* which will win the premiership, not the one with the star names. All 15 players must play their part. But the Italian press obviously thinks the overseas stars win the games, or lose them. Little mention is made of the local players and this unfortunately makes them try things on their own with renewed deter-mination to make the headlines! They end up thinking it is a game for individual achievements. You can tell them that if one of the 15 players does not contribute, there is a missing link until you are blue in the face, but they still return to this basic desire for individual glory.

Another misconception among Italian players is that as soon as they leave their home town or city, they are doomed to lose. They tell you quite cheerfully that the opposition will play much better because they will be at home and the crowd will be right behind them, too. They almost admit they are scared to go to some of these away matches. You try telling them to have confidence in themselves, that it is just another rugby field with the same shaped ball, that it is still 15 against 15; all to no avail.

The two major factors lacking throughout Italian rugby are discipline and concentration. They lack the discipline to concentrate on a game for the full 80 minutes. They will do it for 20 minutes, but then forget about what they are supposed to be doing and why they are there! They easily get frustrated and distracted. It is a pity, because there are some Italian rugby players with an awful lot of ability. If it could all be harnessed together in the national side with the right attitude, then Italy would become a force. But as individuals they all have different ideas on how to play the game and what they should be doing. The result is largely chaotic.

Another national rugby characteristic is a desire to bash each other as hard as possible at all times. I ordered a load of tackle bags when I was over in England in 1989, and were they needed! For the Italians, there seems to be no differentiating between hammering down opponents in a match or just doing it gently when it comes to your team-mates in training. At least tackle bags offered some hope of channelling that aggression properly. However, I remain sceptical: I suspect they will still try and kill each other in training matches!

Somehow, I doubt whether the game will ever really develop in the country. I offer that assessment because I feel that the Italian committee men who run the game are not that interested in seeing it go anywhere in particular. They are basically happy for the game to meander along without threatening to make any major strides. Those committee guys make their little money out of it all and that keeps them content. There is a chronic shortage of real vision and long-term planning. The players, too, earn a certain amount, enough to keep them happy and interested, but no central driving force really exists to expand the game. Rugby is badly in need of promotion throughout the country, but the Italian Federation is not organising that. There is a crying need for someone to have a go with rugby in Italy, not just to let it slumber, which is what is happening at present

A television company bought the rights to screen rugby in Italy but they have little idea. You'll see a match like France versus England in the Five Nations Championship, but halfway through they will break off to show

On a wing and a prayer: playing Rugby League for the Queanbeyan Blues Under-9s.

BOB THOMAS SPORTS PHOTOGRAPHY

COLORSPORT

Moments from our 1984 Grand Slam tour of the UK and Ireland. *Above left:* On the charge against England. (L-R) Simon Poidevin, me, England's Nick Stringer and Mark Ella. *Below left:* The pushover try ... gave an early warning of the impending decline in Welsh rugby. ...*e right:* Congratulating Mark Ella on his try against Scotland. He scored a try in every international of the tour. *Below right:* Beginning the Grand Slam celebrations in the dressing-room at Murrayfield with Mark Ella and Andrew Slack.

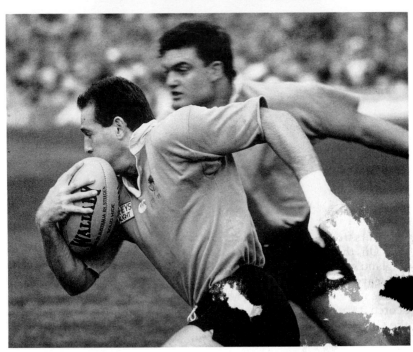

tha

Abo ng ome of my favou e teams. *Above left:* Randwick – the world. *Below left:* On the break for New South Wales agai ne 1989 Lions. *Above right:* My current Italian club, Amatori Milano. *Below right:* The English Barbarians.

Three players whose loss to Australian Rugby Union has been incalculable. *Above:* Ricky Stuart, who turned professional virtually before his Union career had even begun, would surely have been a key member of the Wallaby side for ten years. *Below:* Mark Ella, who retired after our 1984 Grand Slam tour, playing alongside Michael O'Connor, who bowed out in 1982.

Technique at the top. *Above:* Balance in the swerve defeats England's Rory Underwood in the Australians' match against the North of England in 1984. *Below:* A fingertip flick gets the ball away before Tomasi Cama arrives in our 1987 Hong Kong Sevens game with Fiji.

Sun, sea, sand and the life of leisure pictured above would be ideal for me. However, hard work in a tough training session is more usual.

some cycling or tennis. Then they go back to the rugby for a few minutes late in the game. That is hopeless, an absolute joke.

During the past decade, you could have seen some of the finest players in the world game plying their skills in Italian rugby. And what a list (with apologies to those I have unintentionally omitted): Mark Ella, Naas Botha, John Kirwan, Roger Gould, Frano Botica, Mike Brewer, Craig Green, Gary Whetton, Jeff Miller and many others; great players with enormous talents. They should have been used a great deal more than has been the case to spread the rugby message. Little effort appears to be made to get into the schools to promote rugby: that area seems to be largely a wasteland. In Milan three years ago, for example, there were no junior teams at all playing rugby. Now we have Under-13s, Under-15s, Under-17s and Under-19s, all created by the former Milan coach, Guy Pardies, a Frenchman. The Milan club had to attract these youngsters directly – the schools do not seem able to be persuaded away from their total dedication to soccer.

Basic training films should be shown and used, so that everyone is then playing the same kind of rugby. Coaches ought to be examined on their credentials and abilities; too many coaches in the Italian game are just not good enough. I see continuity of playing style as an absolute must for the game's future. You cannot have so many different methods used: at times, some seem to be playing a different game and that is plain daft.

Some of the coaching is beyond the belief of most people associated with the game. I will give you an example. I went to see some Under-15 lads training a year or so ago in Milan, and the guy in charge had them throwing the ball *forward* while some lad was tackling them. I sat on the sidelines, scratching my head and wondering whether I was going mad. I said to the coach, 'What on earth value does this actually have?' He replied, in a tone of voice which seemed to indicate that he was surprised to be asked, that it was to get the lads used to passing the ball and being tackled. But why throw the ball forward every time when that is totally contrary to the most basic law of the game? He didn't seem to have an answer for that one.

So I explained a few things to him, and he said: 'You come here and take training for these lads now. You teach them good'. But that is not the answer. I believe that almost all the overseas players who go to Italy would be more than willing to help, and indeed have a considerable input. But we are not qualified coaches, and they are what is needed. We should just sit and watch and, if it is helpful, occasionally offer advice. But if you do suggest something, they expect you to turn up and take over the entire training programme. And anyway, if the kids train only once a week, they forget what they have been taught. That is why it would be so valuable to spread the game into the schools. They could play it there as well as with the clubs then.

The background restraint to this constant struggle for impetus is soccer, the sport which undermines everything rugby achieves in the country. And the money therein. There are such vast sums involved in the game nowadays that all the kids want to do is to become full-time professional players. In 1990, it was rumoured that some 12-year-old kid had been discovered who was destined to become the best player in the world one day. Clubs were said to be scrapping each other like warring dingoes in the night to get their hands on him. His value was being discussed in terms of millions of lire – at the age of 12! *That* is rugby's problem in Italy.

Reading all this, you might think there are quite enough barriers to the development of the game in Italy already, but there is one more. The standard of refereeing in the country is probably lower than that of the coaching, which is saying something. I have played in matches in Italy, invariably when we have been away from home, in which we have been cheated out of a win. I make no excuses for that accusation because without doubt, it is perfectly true to say such a thing. It is so infuriating to play under these incompetent officials because you just do not have a clue where they learned their so-called knowledge of the laws. In one match in the 1989-90 season six players from our team had their names taken, myself included.

The serious aspect of this is that it is a huge impediment to the advancement and improvement of the game. Players lose heart if they are refereed like that. In turn, the referees themselves become frustrated because they don't know what is happening or see things which do not exist, irritating the players even more. And once that happens with Italian players you have a whole lot more than just a rugby match on your hands. They will destroy the whole game with their petulance and reactions.

The star man, the overseas player, is a popular target for these joke referees. He is usually penalised for offences that don't even exist and then the whole team becomes frustrated. I have suffered this time and again in Italian rugby. The wrong players are sent off for offences and bookings are frequent. Then, a week later, you get the Italian Federation on the telephone, announcing that you are suspended for a week or two. The system is a farce, and that is another reason why I wonder whether Italian rugby will ever improve.

There is a desperate need to show anyone in the country who might be interested some of the basics of the game. Television could do this well, especially with many world-class players in the country. Basic skills should be taught and then shown: how to pass, how to kick and swerve the ball; how to drop-kick, place-kick, ruck and maul, scrummage. It would enable people who don't know rugby to understand something of what the game is about. When a club game is televised, it is frequently a poor one, often from the Second Division, which turns out to bore the trousers off everyone. That is no advertisement for the sport. They must realise that we, the foreign players, are there and willing to help; we want to assist them. Rugby is not being promoted properly and yet money is still given by an overall body in Italian sport to assist with the development of all sports. You wonder where it goes and what is done with it. My great fear concerning rugby in Italy, a country I love deeply, is that in five or even ten years' time there will not be that much difference from today. That would be tragic. But I foresee a situation in which the system will be perpetuated: today's juniors will have come through but they won't really have mastered the basics of the game, even when they reach the senior side. And no one will really care or bother too much about that. The game cannot advance if that is the case. The Italian Federation is partly to blame for the standard of the game in the country. They do not support or help rugby at all. The standard of refereeing is shocking but no one really addresses that aspect: it's always the players who are held responsible for making the mistakes, but it is partly because the referees don't know the rules. Referees should be judged on their performances, like players are. In a recent game, one of our players slipped over in the mud. There was no opposition within five metres of the player so he passed the ball off the ground and the referee penalised him. After the game, I asked the referee why he had made that decision. He responded that nobody on the ground can play the ball. He said it was in the rules, but I disagree: the rules state that a tackled player cannot play the ball on the ground. But if I was at full-back, caught the ball and slipped over, does that mean I cannot pass the ball off the ground? Plainly that is nonsense and just one of the frustrations of rugby in Italy.

On a lighter note, I mentioned Giacomo and Vittorio as Pixie and Dixie. These two great friends love playing jokes on each other and on me. Giacomo is a dentist, and one day I was in his surgery where he was fixing my front teeth. I had known him for two years, and knew what he was capable of, both as a dentist and practical joker. He told me to put my thumb on my chin and press hard in an upward direction for a few minutes. Well, being an intelligent threequarter, I thought this was very strange, so I quickly pulled my thumb away and found that it was stuck. I turned round and saw Giacomo almost crying with laughter. He had put some sort of glue on my chin and my thumb was stuck for a few seconds until I really pulled hard to release it! I'm happy to say that my teeth are fixed and I still have both hands free to play rugby. Happily, I still have a few years left in Italy to get back at him, too!

CHAPTER
— 4 —

THE NEW WALLABY

Whatever else anyone might feel moved to accuse me of, I doubt whether the charge of predictability could ever be levelled at me. If you glance at the career records of most of the game's leading players, you will find, generally speaking, a fairly consistent story from the days when they first played Rugby Union: appeared in junior school team, then school 1st XV, on to university followed by club and then international rugby. It is a path well trodden by young men the world over who appear for their respective countries. In my case, there were a few diversions from the accepted route to the international arena.

I didn't start playing rugby until I was ten. I was at school in Queanbeyan, which is in New South Wales, near the Australian Capital Territory, and we used to play Union on Saturdays and League on Sundays. That suited me fine; the more sport the better as far as I was concerned. It also meant there was even less time to spend on my homework, which was another arrangement tailor-made for me! The rule at our school was that sport was not compulsory, but if you wanted to participate there was plenty of scope. So at one stage, I was playing three winter sports: Rugby Union, League and also Aussie Rules. It was no wonder I had so little time for my studies!

However, when I was 12, my career in Rugby Union was cut off in its prime. As a kid, I played in the five-eighth position of the team and no one outside me ever got the ball (so what's new?). This did not concern me unduly until one day my Dad came to watch me play in some club match for the Queanbeyan Whites. All these years later, I cannot recall every aspect of what happened. But we were playing in this game at home and were winning pretty comfortably. Somehow, from a position of command, we made an absolute mess of it and ended up losing. And it quickly became clear who Dad blamed for that state of affairs.

He called me aside afterwards and said: 'That's it. You're not playing Union any more'. I was dumbfounded. I thought he must be joking, but he meant it all right. To this day, I still don't know exactly why he banned me from playing the game, but I figured at the time that he thought I was responsible for our defeat, probably because I never passed the ball to anyone else. I wanted to do it all myself in those days; score the tries, make all the great runs and catch the eye. What a show-off!

By this time, our family was six strong, a typical Italian family. My brother, Mario, is four years older than me. He used to play Rugby League for Queanbeyan Blues but gave that away when he was younger. Today, he is very knowledgeable on all sports. He can tell you who is the leading wicket-taker, who has scored most runs in a season and, football-wise, he knows all the players. He enjoys life to the full. I also have two younger sisters, Lisa who is three years younger than me, and Corrina, five years younger than me. They both work in Canberra and were both very, very good at softball and netball. They play touch rugby in the summer months and enjoy the participation that goes with any sport. But now their time is occupied by my nephews and nieces: Lisa has a young boy, Terry, who loves Rugby Union and supports the local team, Canberra Raiders. Who in Canberra doesn't? Corrina has two girls, Taleana and Antoinette, and a little boy named Dwayne. Most of her time is taken up by the three of them. So you can see that when I go home I have my hands full. It's good to catch up with them when I do get home which, as I have said, is not very often, due to the demands of Italy, Randwick and Test match rugby.

I think my father likes the fact that I can now speak Italian. We sometimes have a chat in the language on the telephone and he enjoys news of his brothers and sisters. He hopes to return to Italy after the 1991 World Cup for a visit. One particular highlight, for me and probably for him, was when I sent home a letter in Italian for the first time. I'm not sure it was the best Italian ever written, but he appreciated the effort and I liked writing it. My Mum, who has Irish links, still lives in the street where she was born in Queanbeyan. I believe my sporting attributes came from my mother's side because her brothers and sisters were very, very good sportsmen and women. Tommy and Johnny, my uncles, were excellent Australian Rules players, representing the Queanbeyan Tigers. One of Mum's sisters, Dawn, surprised me by coming to Sydney with Mum and Dad in 1990 to watch the Test we played against France, my 50th Test.

My Mum and Dad and sisters have seen several Tests in Sydney. But my Dad gets so frustrated: he likes to see a team run the ball and cannot understand why any side playing Union should kick the ball for the whole match. Especially Australia. After the 1990 Grand Final between Randwick and Eastern Suburbs, my friend Daryl, my father and I went back to the Randwick club. Bob Dwyer was there, and said to my father: 'Why don't you go home and try to make another David?' I think my father replied: 'You must be joking. One is enough!'

I miss my family a lot, especially in the last couple of years when I have been spending six months or so in Italy. I miss seeing my nephews and nieces growing up, so when I managed to get home for Christmas 1990, which was about the first Christmas I'd had at home in six years, it was an enjoyable time. However, I would like to have known and understood my family better than I do, in the context of sharing and remembering the fun times, the good times and even ordinary moments which I feel we have all missed out on. Part of the reason for that has been the fact that after almost every big tour, I have gone straight to Italy for the rest of the northern hemisphere season, so I have never had the chance to tell my parents and family about the tour, the great characters of the team and the individual moments. That has been a loss to me and, because I am away so much, I am not as close to my parents as I would have liked.

However, it's nice to know that my family supports me in the decisions I have made, although Dad now and then reminds me about the huge League offers I have had or asks why I did not play tennis or golf, sports in which so much money is involved. Without their support over the years, I would have missed a lot. Although I might not get home that often, it is a good feeling to know that I have that base available to me. I'm afraid I'm the world's worst at remembering birthdays and anniversaries, as my poor mother knows only too well. In 1989, during the Wallaby tour of France, I couldn't remember whether my Mum's birthday was on 6 November or 6 December. To be on the safe side, while we were in Grenoble I found a florist's and sent her some flowers the week before 6 November. When the day arrived I telephoned Mum to wish her a happy birthday. When I was reminded that it wasn't until 6 December, actually, I wished her a happy 50th birthday, anyway, whenever it was. But even that wasn't right, I'm afraid – Mum explained that she was only 49! Still, I suppose it is the thought that counts!

I feel very sorry for them sometimes because when Australia have lost a Test or I did not personally play very well, my poor family are the ones to bear the brunt of it. Dad is given a very hard time at work, and there have been a few occasions when my brother has been in fights just because he is my brother. Sad, isn't it, the way the Australian public treat their sportsmen? While we are on the subject of my family and friends, I would like to say how grateful I am to all those with whom I have been close over the years in the little town of Queanbeyan – they have helped me get where I am today.

It has been a pleasure and an honour for me to have learned so much in my younger days, because they have really been of enormous benefit to me in my subsequent life.

From 12 right through to 17, I hardly played Union. I think I was involved in perhaps three or four odd games a year, but those few aside, it was strictly League and Aussie Rules. It didn't worry me greatly, because I just assumed I would stay with League throughout my career. After all, in large parts of Australia, it was and still is far more popular than Union. So the absence of Union from my diary of sporting commitments was no cause for major concern – I accepted it as a fact of life and got on with doing as well as I could in League. At 16, I gave away all football and played golf for one year, winning the ACT schoolboy championship and coming second in the club championship at Queanbeyan B grade. I was playing off a handicap of 12 or 13 at that time and was seriously considering taking up golf as a career.

But, at 17, I decided to go back to Union, mainly for reasons I have already discussed but also because I didn't think I had the right mental approach for golf. It was too hard for me, a very demanding sport! By now, I had left school and played my Rugby Union at the Queanbeyan Whites club, in fourth grade. We won the premiership, the first time in the club's history that a fourth grade side had won it. Even to this day, I still look back on that year and can say with all honesty that I have never had more enjoyment from a year's rugby than in that season in fourth grade. After a single season with the fourths I was moved up into first grade. After two seasons at that level, in 1981 I got into the Australian Under-21 squad, and went on their tour of New Zealand. We were beaten 37-7 by the young All Blacks, who included some future stars in Gary Whetton, Albert Anderson, Arthur Stone, Grant Fox, Kieran Crowley and maybe others. In the same year, I was given a Wallaby trial. What an experience that was.

All the big-name stars were chosen – Glen Ella, Paul McLean, Michael O'Connor, Greg Cornelsen and John Hipwell – and the bolters, the kids, made up the other team. We looked at the side we were up against in that trial and thought, 'This is absurd. We are going to get flogged'. So what happened? We got flogged! No fairytale ending there, I'm afraid. The senior side was just too powerful and experienced for us and overran our young team. I did manage to score a try, in the last minute, from a cross-field kick which I caught, stepping inside Glen Ella to cross the line. I have rubbished Glen for his defence ever since that incident!

That trial match took place just before the Wallabies departed for the UK on their 1981 tour of Britain. My try did me no good; I missed out on selection for that trip and, frankly, I wasn't in the least surprised. I never thought I was even in the frame. There were some very famous Wallaby names knocking around at that time for selection, players like Hawker,

Moon, McLean, Slack and Gould. I never even remotely considered the possibility of getting a look-in among that sort of company – I had only just turned 19, and was surprised even to get a Wallaby trial at that time.

The 1981 Wallabies disappointed on their tour. They lost to England, Scotland and Wales and their only Test victory was over Ireland. The party which had set out with such hopes returned bitterly dejected. The match against England at Twickenham on 2 January 1982 heralded a momentous year in many respects for Australian rugby, and for me, too. The domestic season saw Scotland on tour in Australia, stunning the Wallabies by beating them 12-7 in the first Test at Ballymore. It was Scotland's first Test win against a major rugby nation in the southern hemisphere. The Australian team had been chosen against the usual background of loud discontent among Queenslanders with the selection of certain New South Wales players, and of similar disagreement among New South Wales men about the choice of Queenslanders. Sitting well away from all this down in the ACT, I honestly wondered how it was that Australia ever won a rugby match, given the innate rivalry between players and supporters from the two states.

The competitive element was all right when the two states played each other, but not when the players were wearing Australian jerseys against an overseas team. At Ballymore in that first Test, Australia's five-eighth Mark Ella was booed by his own countrymen, purely because he came from New South Wales. That was unforgivable: that kind of attitude leaves me bewildered.

Well, after defeat in the first Test the Australian selectors completely changed the team. Out went the Ellas, in came Roger Gould and Paul McLean, the Queenslanders the Ballymore crowd had wanted included in the first place, and it worked like a dream. In the second Test Gould scored two tries, McLean kicked five penalty goals and three conversions and Australia won 33-9.

Exactly 14 days later, the Wallabies were due to play the first match of their New Zealand tour against Taranaki in New Plymouth. It was thought that a pretty established, solid Wallaby party would head across the Tasman to take on the All Blacks. I could only guess at the eventual line-up of the touring party, but I was certain of one thing: my name would not be on the list. There was no reason for me to be there; Australia had some high quality wings: Brendan Moon, Peter Grigg and Mick Martin, and others, like Michael Hawker, who could play on the wing as well as in the centre. Then, however, the sky fell in: the news came through that ten Test players, nine of them from Queensland, had made themselves unavailable for the tour. Pressure of work or the lack of time in previous months for study were the reasons given, but whatever the factors, the Wallaby selectors had a hand grenade lobbed into their selection meeting. Just two members of the Test pack which beat Scotland at Sydney could make the tour.

When someone told me I was in the party, I rubbished them, thinking they were having me on! Even when I read it in the newspaper, it took some time to persuade me that it wasn't a misprint. Had someone forecast that I would not only make the tour but play as many games as any other member of the squad (nine) and appear in all the Tests (three), I'd have suspected some malfunction of the brain. But, believe it or not – and I certainly couldn't at the time – at the age of 19 all those things happened to me. It was the most exciting time of my life. Can anyone imagine how a 19-year-old with no track record at all in top-class rugby, felt when he was chosen? Of course, I was young and I was stupid, but I loved it all! And it was a very different pressure on us. True, every Australian side that plays New Zealand wants to do well and win, whatever the sport. As with the Kiwis and the Kangaroos in Rugby League, the river of confrontation runs deep. However, no one expected us to achieve much at all. Before we even left Australia, enough excuses had been trotted out about our inexperience and the loss of so many class players that you could hardly feel the slightest pressure. But there was another factor involved, and that was personal pride. Believe me, no one should ever underestimate that quality on the rugby field.

My first game of that tour came against Manawatu, in the New Zealand North Island town of Palmerston North (some Kiwis call it a city, but sorry, folks – Sydney and Auckland are cities, not Palmerston North!) on 31 July 1982. It was the first time I ever wore the green and gold shirt of a senior Australian rugby team and I can still recall moments from that match all these years later. I scored a try and kicked three goals from five attempts in our 26-10 win, but it was obvious how much of a bolter I was. When the *Rothmans Australian Rugby Yearbook* came out the following year, one of the tries was credited to some bloke called D. Caampese! I don't know who he was.

I played in the next game, too, against Hawke's Bay at Napier and, two matches later, was chosen for the first Test. Again, it was cold-cloth-on-the-head and sit-down-to-absorb-the-shock time! My first Test match for Australia was not a very good one, either for me or the team. I beat Stu Wilson, the All Black wing, a few times, on a couple of occasions by employing the goose-step. So much has been made of that fact over the years that it has been blown up out of all proportion. I had done the goose-step several times before in my career; it wasn't a new trick. And anyway, it had been part of my game for some years, since I was eight years old, in fact. I used it as a kid and other people had employed it, too, especially a Rugby League player I had once seen. But when it worked in a Test against New Zealand, everyone went overboard. Crazy, really.

The goose-step is something you cannot work on, it just happens and you know it is there for occasional use. Some people believe it is a high-risk tactic in terms of the danger of pulling a hamstring, but I have never found that. If you do it halfway through a game or later on, you will be all right. Of course, if you try it in the first five minutes before you have warmed up properly, then you are inviting problems. For people to talk about only that aspect of my game when other parts were unbelievably undisciplined was blinkered. As Mark Ella, our captain, remarked afterwards, I might have been a good player but I was an individual. I had no discipline, was very young and wanted to do everything myself. Mark was spot-on in his verdict.

I remember that in the first half of that Test match at Christchurch, Roger Gould had a kick charged down and I went to pick it up one-handed . . . and knocked on. In a Test match! Then, in the second half, we got the ball and ran it from our own line. Gould gave me the ball and there was no one in front of me except Allan Hewson, the All Black full-back. I tried to change hands and dropped the ball. Maybe I have always been a bit that way; unpredictable to the end.

Even before the tour had begun my unpredictability had shown itself. I had played for Australia Under-21s against New Zealand Under-21s as the curtain-raiser to the second Test of the Scotland tour in Australia. I got the ball, beat the opposing wing and chipped the full-back to score. It would have been a lot easier if I had drawn my opponent and given the ball to our wing. But that was the kind of guy I was then – I was just trying to impress. I'm not particularly proud of my play in those days. I guess I half felt I could do it all, like so many young kids. But I will say that I learned much on that 1982 tour of New Zealand about discipline and the need to be part of a team.

Anyway, despite my goose-stepping, we lost that first Test 23-16. I did score a try, but not until two minutes from the end when we were trailing 23-12. So in the context of that particular match it had little relevance, but I would say it was of lasting value to Australian rugby in the years to come. That is because of the way it was scored. Mark Ella cross-kicked a long ball to me on the left wing, I gathered and touched down wide out. It was probably one of the early demonstrations of the partnership, the understanding between Mark and myself, which was to bear fruit on many, many occasions for Australia, Randwick and finally for Amatori in Milan.

Our special understanding in years of rugby together derived simply from the way we both wanted to play the game. It might all have looked like off-the-cuff stuff, with decisions taken instantly, but it wasn't always like that. Mark would say, OK, we have a scrum; the first move we do will be this, than we will go blindside if we get the ball again and then see. Where

Mark was so special, what made him great, was that a lot of players think in terms of only one phase. My view, and Mark concurred in this, was that you should always try to imagine what was going to happen two phases further on down the field. Then you could work out where you should be and that meant your value to the side was greatly enhanced. Call it what you will, reading the game, if you like, but it was the exercise of attempting to forecast where the play would be. It was not always easy, of course, and frequently we would be wrong.

Mark was a whole lot better at doing this than me because he could look beyond the first and even second phase to third-phase situations. That was a rare gift. I just tried to follow him and see what was happening and why he took up certain positions. Frankly, I was intrigued on many occasions. The other Ella brothers, Glen and Gary, also had this talent and that was why they were so magical when they played together. They could touch the ball five times in a movement just because they knew where they were going to be. They had a good combination and didn't have to look, they were just there. That is where our understanding came from. I followed and Mark knew I would be there.

No two players are the same, and of course we were very different, Mark and I. I could never be the same as him, much as I would have liked to be. Even in Italy in the final season he played, I was still amazed at some of the things he could do. The first time I saw Mark Ella play was in 1981, when Australia beat New Zealand at home in the Bledisloe Cup, a coveted and all too rare achievement. A year later, I was playing alongside him on the Wallaby tour of New Zealand, when he was captain.

Glen and Gary Ella were also on that tour and I found them all easy-going characters. If you ever want a favour they will look after you. They are the world's greatest guys, and when it came to rugby they just wanted to enjoy themselves. If you are born with a talent such as theirs, then you want to use it in the best possible way but also to enjoy it. And we sure had some great fun together. Even in the final games Mark played in company with Gary for Randwick, we had some fun on the field. We had all got older but rugby remained a game for pleasure, for enjoyment with the pursuit of victory in no way tarnished by the desire to have fun.

So we lost that first Test in New Zealand, just, but we won the next one. And the whole of New Zealand, and perhaps much of Australia, too, sat up in amazement at how a bunch of kids had toppled a team of mighty players. We led 19-3 at half-time, having plundered a gale force wind in our favour in the first half at Athletic Park, Wellington. After two early Roger Gould penalty goals, I got through and found Mark Ella close by in support. Gould took it on, I backed him up and gave Gary Ella the scoring pass. Hewson then kicked a penalty for the All Blacks to close the gap to 10-3, but another Gould penalty followed by a try I finished off, but for which I was indebted to seven other guys who did all the approach work, made it 17-3 and Gould converted superbly. We knew the Blacks would come at us with the wind behind them after half-time. But we kept them down to 13 points, hanging on through a nerve-racking last eight minutes until the final whistle sounded. New Zealand 16, Australia 19 – and I had been a part of it. I could scarcely believe it all.

The secret of our Test win was the fact that we ran the ball. Bob Dwyer had always said that as long as we got 40 per cent of the ball we could beat the All Blacks. Well, the forwards gave us the pill and we used it. I think New Zealand expected us to kick all the time, to use the strong wind. But we had a good back line and used it. Again, this was not just off-the-cuff stuff – we had worked hard on all the moves. You have to have that discipline; you cannot go out in a Test match and just chuck it around and hope it will come off.

I think we were still partying when we went out to meet Bay of Plenty at Rotorua four days later. Whatever the reason, we were flogged 40-16. Someone told me afterwards that I'd done well because I scored two tries and landed a conversion. I said, 'Please be serious'.

I was disappointed with New Zealand's tactics at Wellington. They seemed content to kick the ball through for the wings to chase rather than giving them a chance to keep the ball in their hands. But perhaps our first-half play had intimidated them. Personally, I thought it was the All Blacks who were the intimidating side then, and I still do today. They seem to know they can get away with a fair bit so they do it. In those days I wasn't the greatest tackler in the game – I'm still not, so not much has changed, has it? – and I didn't do a lot of tackling. I didn't get caught in too many rucks, either, but I still knew it was a real, physical experience playing against those guys.

We knew New Zealand had changed their attitude when we reached Eden Park, Auckland for the third and deciding Test of the series. A crowd of 52,000 was crammed inside and they saw Allan Hewson win the match for the Blacks by scoring 26 of their points in a 33-18 win. Hewson scored a try, kicked two conversions, dropped a goal and booted five penalty goals. It was a new world record for a Test match. Yet it was Australia who had fired the first shots when Roger Gould scored a superb try and converted it in the first 120 seconds of the game. Our lead soon disappeared, yet we were back in front, by 15-12, at half-time. But in the second half the All Black forwards took charge and won the match. Out in the Wallaby back line, we almost forgot what it felt like to have the ball in our hands.

Hindsight makes experts of everyone, of course, but even at the time I respected that New Zealand side. Now, if I were to judge them alongside the All Black teams I have seen since, I would still put them above almost all others. They had some fantastic players, people like Graham Mourie, Stu Wilson and Bernie Fraser, who were a great pair of wings, Dave Loveridge at half-back and forwards like Andy Haden, Gary Knight, Mark Shaw and Murray Mexted. To me, it was a better side than the All Black team which won the 1987 World Cup and enjoyed such a long run unbeaten. There was greater skill individually, a greater capacity for flair and high quality throughout that 1982 team. The World Cup-winning side five years later was extremely fit and functional, and it had a phenomenal goal-kicker in Grant Fox, who has won countless matches off his own bat. But it lacked outstanding individual performers of the quality of Mourie and Stu Wilson. But then, that may reflect the path rugby has taken in recent years, away from the individuals and towards a more functional unit. Mourie was a superb leader and an outstanding character. In his quiet, unobtrusive manner, he was one of the finest flank forwards I have ever seen in the game.

Mexted had enormous presence as a No 8, and for me he was a better all-round player than Wayne Shelford has ever been, because he had much more skill. Bill Osborne and Steve Pokere were the first-choice centres. They were a magnificent combination and complemented each other. Pokere had loads of class while Osborne was a good, solid, rugged competitor who could offer the variation to Pokere's sleight of hand.

It has been a fascinating experience to see how rugby has changed over the years, and the experience of touring New Zealand has always been very good. It might not have been my favourite country to tour, but it did force me to concentrate on my game, which was good for me. It was especially valuable to go there as a youngster with the 1982 Wallabies; it set high standards which I realised I had to attain if I was to make the grade in international rugby. But I would say that the standard of rugby over there in 1986 and 1990 was not as good as in 1982. In more recent years, some players who have been past their best have appeared in All Black sides and that has surprised me. However, I should put all this in context: the bottom line is that you never get a bad All Black team. The commitment is always fanatical and it's always the devil of a job to finish ahead of them, whoever is playing for them. Most things change in life, but the consistent quality of New Zealand rugby teams seems to go on forever.

I doubt very much whether you would find the situation in New Zealand rugby that I have noticed has been creeping into the Australian game at Test match level. When I first got into the Australian team at 19, I listened and didn't say a word. When the coach or the senior players spoke or offered advice, I took it without a murmur. I figured it was all part of the learning process. After all, you are bound to learn from the experienced guys. But these days I find the young guys in the team are trying to tell me what to do. If you try to make any suggestions they start to argue. What that says to me is that today there are a lot of players who think they are a bit special when in reality they are not at all. If you are going to become a good player in Test rugby, then the best way to go about it is to learn from others who have been through it, not to make out that you know it all and can tell them!

After I had played my first game for Australia against Manawatu I thought I was the king, but that ludicrous belief was quickly shattered by the older guys around me. They told me where to get off. Bob Dwyer and the captain, Mark Ella, said quite clearly that I had to concentrate and play a lot harder. What I thought had been a good performance had not been that flash at all. You have to say, 'right, that game is finished – now I must try to improve', not think to yourself, 'I'm made, I have arrived, so I will take it easy here because I know I can play well'. There were guys back at my club, too, telling me where to get off in those days, after I had gone back and started to speak loudly about my ideas on the game. Australians are good at that – they tell you when to shut up, and quickly. That was good for me, just what I needed. It shrank my head.

Terry McLean, writing in the *New Zealand Herald* at the conclusion of that 1982 tour, said: 'The one lack of Wallaby rugby is forwards of real strength in physical confrontation. Beyond that, the brilliance. Mark Ella, sublime in handling and knowing where to be; Campese, who could side-step his way out of a sealed paper bag [I must try that some day!]; Gould, surely one of the greatest punt-kickers in all of rugby history; . . . Gary Ella, of the wonderful, natural talent; Hawker, perhaps too much inclined to go on his own, but strikingly dangerous; Phillip Cox, a scrum-half who served his passes and made his runs and came back for more; Chris Roche, a flanker who stood as high in the sky as the eye of a baby elephant and who weighed about a quarter as much, but who tracked the field at the speed of a Deerfoot; Simon Poidevin and "Rowdy" Lucas, who so well supported Roche; Steve Williams and Duncan Hall, who between them might have won the final Test if Hall hadn't had his tour ended by a brutal boot in the back in the second; the other forwards and backs who, like the smile of a cat, emanated at amazing places and impossible times to carry on the ball. Bravo the Wallabies'.

I think he quite liked us.

When we returned to Australia, it was finals time in the Canberra competition. Queanbeyan had worked hard to get into the finals and had won their way into the Grand Final. A week after my return from New Zealand I was playing full-back for Queanbeyan in a competition in which we had not won a premiership since 1969. We won that Grand Final, but during the game I was heckled every time I got the ball and the crowd accused me of losing the third Test against New Zealand. A small price to pay for fame! We also won the Grand Final in 1983 and 1984. In 1984, when we won 29-12, I scored all 29 points, which I am sure remains a record! That day, playing at full-back once again, I scored four tries, two conversions and three penalty goals.

In 1983, I played in four Test matches for Australia prior to the close season tour to France and Italy. The first was against the USA at Sydney, a match which we won in a canter, so much so that I scored four tries myself, the most I have ever achieved in a Test match. But I don't regard that as a great achievement; American rugby in those days was a long way removed from the New Zealand standard. The tries I had scored in the Tests against the All Blacks at Christchurch and Wellington the previous year made me infinitely more proud. We then played two Tests against Argentina in Australia before meeting New Zealand for the Bledisloe Cup at Sydney, a match we lost amid great dismay in our country. The lad who was to score 29 points in a Grand Final the following year missed four shots at goal from four attempts (two penalty goals and two conversions), and we lost 16-8, two tries to one in our favour, against the mighty All Blacks. I felt like kicking myself, but I would probably have missed!

Off we went afterwards on the tour to France and Italy where, I think it is fair to say, we never really captured the great flair and spirit which had been a hallmark of our New Zealand tour a year earlier. Some influential players from the All Black series were missing; men like Hawker, Cox, Grigg in the backs and, up front, Meadows, Walker and Lucas. Besides, touring France in those days was no sort of pleasure. There were some guys on the tour who had been to France before and returned reluctantly because they knew that tours there could be difficult affairs. Perhaps they communicated their feelings to the rest of us.

Whatever the reason, it was not a tour to savour. The French softened us up in the first match by picking a team of thugs to knock the hell out of us. That was quite usual; you saw the same old ferocious faces in almost all the matches against what the French term a 'French Selection XV'. The idea, of course, was to weaken our commitment so that by the time the Test matches came along we would be physically weary and none too keen on the battering. Well, Australians can handle a bit of stick and we did. But even so, we did not regain the flowing play which had been so spectacular at times in New Zealand.

We lost two provincial games, drew another and won four. In the Tests, we drew 15-15 at Clermont-Ferrand but then lost the second international 15-6 at Parc des Princes. It was never a great tour, and the referees did not help. I have been in matches in France where you could see the guy in charge making decisions which amounted to blatant cheating. And, with that attitude, you wonder why touring teams went there at all. I have to say that by the time we went back in 1989 it seemed better. The trouble that time was that the Australian Rugby Union seemed to have been involved in a trade-off. Apparently, the idea was that the Australians would agree to a French request to play a lot of night matches on their tour if the French accepted an Australian proposal to play three Test matches on their tour of Australia in 1990. The idea of playing night games was, of course, absurd. What kind of preparation would it be for two Test matches, which would be played on Saturday afternoons, to have night games everywhere else on the tour? But, once again, money was at the root of it all.

The Australians wanted the extra revenue from a third Test with the French in Sydney. And the French got their night games as soon as they agreed to that third Test. Somewhere, lost in the middle of that cosy little arrangement, were a group of players who could have screamed in frustration at the idea of playing so many night games. But, as usual, we were never consulted. The itinerary was just handed to us after all the horse-trading and we had to get on with it. No one ever asks the players what they think; it is standard practice in this game.

All this meant that in 1990 we played three Test matches in three weeks against France, followed a week later by another Test against the USA and, within two more weeks, we had played two of New Zealand's toughest provincial sides, Waikato and Auckland, as well as the All Blacks in the first Test. If that was not a schedule designed by a maniac, I don't know what would be. Never again should Australia play a full Test against the USA in those circumstances – it should have been an Australian B side. There are two reasons for this: first, we beat the USA by almost 60 points in a one-sided rout and secondly, and much more importantly, Jason Little cracked a bone in his ankle during the match, and as a result missed the tour of New Zealand which started a week later. This was ridiculous.

Back in 1983, we had not found the French particularly friendly. Andrew Slack, the Queenslander who was to lead the Wallabies on their 1984 Grand Slam tour of Britain and Ireland as successor to Mark Ella, remembered one particular night, after the first Test in Clermont-Ferrand I think it was, when he asked the French captain, Jean-Pierre Rives, something about where the party was to be that night. Rives completely ignored him and turned away. Maybe he didn't understand, perhaps he didn't even hear him; I don't know. But it did not leave a very great impression on the guys in the Australian squad.

I am pleased to say that by 1989 relationships had improved, both at player level and between the respective unions. Players like Serge Blanco had a lot to do with that, for he was widely respected and liked by the players of both sides. You could enjoy time in Serge's company and that is how it should be. Certain other Frenchmen from that recent era were very good company, too; guys like Frank Mesnel and Jean-Baptiste Lafond, the two wonderfully talented players from Racing Club de France, the 1990 French champions.

For the non-French-speaking visitor to France life can be pretty complicated. You can't turn on the television and understand anything; the newspapers make equally little sense. In those circumstances, you need some guys like Mesnel and Lafond to organise things after Test matches, to invite you to a party or two or just generally to be around to help out. Both speak English fluently, an enormous advantage in that situation.

I think it always helps anyone who is overseas on tour to have some local guys prepared to smooth your path. They can show you the ropes, point out the best restaurants and bars or cafés and perhaps assist with any other arrangements. Without those guys, it all becomes a great deal more difficult, so I'd like to say to Frank and Jean-Baptiste, thanks for all your help in recent times, guys. It has been much appreciated.

UK GRAND SLAM

Without too much exaggeration, I think it is fair to say that the trail the 1984 Wallabies blazed through Great Britain and Ireland created effects on the game in that part of the world which are still acknowledged today, years later. In the context of what the Australians achieved on that tour and the shake-up our success gave to British rugby, it was probably *the* most influential tour I have ever been on. It was certainly a wonderful visit which ultimately brought great reward for all our industry and effort.

It is not my intention here to list details of how every try was scored and why each goal was kicked nor to analyse each important movement which took place during our long trip. It is too long ago and, besides, the recounting of individual tries at any great length bores me to tears. I prefer to rake through the effects that tour had, to let people into some of the secrets of the tour; to provide something of an insight into what made us successful, and also to recount some of the lighter moments away from what the public saw at the time.

Our attitude to that tour was encapsulated by what took place, not in the first Test, against England, nor even in the first game, against London Division at Twickenham. You could see us setting out our stall on the very first morning we arrived in London, tired and stiff after the long flight across the world from Sydney. It had been the usual luxurious passage – everyone cramped together down at the back of the plane, six-foot six-inch lock forwards squeezed into seats just about big enough to accommodate nine-year-old children; four of these giants in a row, in the central section of the economy class seating plan, just like you find sardines squashed in a can when you open it up! When this pile of complaining human cargo was disgorged at Heathrow Airport, there was still another hurdle to negotiate. Anyone who has ever flown from Australia to London knows that flights invariably arrive in the early hours of the morning, just in time to catch the morning rush-hour into central London. The queue generally starts at around Heathrow and you lurch into the capital in some bus at about half-a-mile an hour. You think you are never going to reach your hotel.

When we finally arrived at our London base, St Ermin's Hotel around the back of St James's, we had something of a surprise awaiting us. As soon as the press conference, in which the tour management would meet the media, was over we were to be ready for a two-hour training session. This was like making the journey to Mars and finding you were on military duty that morning! Nor was it to be a gentle half-hour's jog to run off the stiffness from the flight. We were booked for a full training programme which was a proper work-out. The Wallabies had landed! It was clever thinking by our coach, Alan Jones, because it emphasised right from the beginning to the guys that they were there to do a job, not just to have a good time. From that day onwards, we were determined to show those people in Britain how to play good rugby.

Our predecessors, the 1981-82 Wallabies under Tony Shaw, had gone away seething with frustration and struggling to banish the sense of failure from the tour. Ireland were the only one of the Home Unions to be beaten by those Wallabies; all the other Tests had been lost, although none by a margin greater than nine points. It was the classic case of what might have been.

We had been aware of all that when we came over. Alan Jones never missed a trick as far as psychology was concerned, and this point had been brought to our attention even before we had left Australia. Our sights had been set, our targets lined up and we felt deep down that we had the ammunition to do the job. And there was another factor: earlier that year, we had met the All Blacks in a three-match series in Australia and let them off the hook, good and proper. We had won the first Test in Sydney and gone 12-0 up in the second in Brisbane. Yet from that highly-promising position, we had somehow contrived to let them escape, not only with a victory in that second Test but eventually in the series: they won the third Test back in Sydney by a single point, 25-24. It was a bitterly disappointing outcome to a series we should have had in our pockets by half-time in the second Test. That salutary lesson had been learned painfully; when you have a team down, finish them off. Show them no mercy; go straight for the clean kill. We had failed to do this in Brisbane and paid a high penalty.

You could talk until midnight about certain incidents involving the English referee in that third Test, and the strangely limited play of the Australian midfield backs, who rarely released the ball out wide. But, at the end of that series, Australia had only themselves to blame for the All Blacks' victory. A great many of us resolved there and then that we would not allow such a thing to happen on the UK tour later that year. The few players on our 1984 UK tour who had been there three years earlier – men like Mark Ella, Roger Gould, Brendan Moon, Chris Roche, Simon Poidevin and Andrew Slack – were all determined not to leave once again as losers. And those guys set the example for the younger ones to follow; in training and in preparation and determination. They showed a businesslike approach to the tour which rubbed off on everyone else.

When you win every Test match on a tour of the UK and Ireland, to become the first-ever touring side from Australia to achieve the mythical 'Grand Slam', then it is probably invidious to pull out a name or two as the stars of the show. By necessity, everyone pulled together and did their bit. The spirit was always fantastic and we helped each other. Slacky was a quiet but inspirational leader and at the other end of the ladder of experience, new caps like Nick Farr-Jones and Michael Lynagh emerged to play crucial roles.

But for me, one man stood out as he did in the eyes of the British and Irish media when they came to write their summaries of the tour. Mark Ella not only became the first Australian ever to score a try in every international on a UK and Ireland tour, but his general play in each Test was of a formidably high standard. When Mark lost the captaincy to Andy Slack, he was bitterly disappointed and upset. But the way Mark played on that 1984 tour in Britain and Ireland probably proved that the decision to relieve him of the leadership had been the correct one. Leading a side always takes something from your individual display because you are always thinking about the team, not your own game. As a captain, you have to try and set the rules for the team, like the Prime Minister for his cabinet, but as an individual you can concentrate exclusively on your own game.

It is my firm belief that, several years later, when Nick Farr-Jones became captain of Australia, his play suffered even though he made a very good captain. Not a lot, but just a bit. Without the burden of the captaincy, I think Mark Ella set out to prove on that 1984 tour that he was one of the world's greatest players. And he did just that, by playing as well as he could.

There was one other person who ensured that Mark Ella played at his absolute best during that tour. It is undoubtedly true to say that no one has got more out of Mark than Alan Jones did on that tour. They were total opposites in character with the added complication that Ella was a Randwick player and Jones a former coach of Manly. Anyone who knows anything about Sydney rugby will know the extent of the rivalry between those two clubs. If you are a British reader, simply substitute Celtic and Rangers, or Arsenal and Tottenham, for Randwick and Manly and you will get the general idea. Mark is an intelligent guy (I have to say that after he paid me so much for being nice to him). He knew what he wanted and what he could do. And perhaps it was the discipline and cohesion that Jones brought to the side which helped release Mark to produce the skills he showed in the context of that team. He not only scored a try himself in each of the Tests on that tour but helped instigate countless others. I don't think Australian rugby has ever really replaced him since his retirement at the end of that tour.

Our first game on that trip was against London Division, a match we won pretty comfortably, by 22-3 and three tries to nil. The match was nothing exceptional, but what was said at the after-match function certainly was. Steve Williams, our vice-captain, had been skipper that day, and after the game we went off to an official dinner in the Rose Room at Twickenham. We walked in, looked down the room and saw the table for the officials – or 'heavies' as the players call them – was about 30 feet long. Not a promising start!

At events like that, you are expected to show your gratitude and say the right things, especially in England, old chap, what, eh? Steve Williams – 'Swill' as his playing colleagues knew him – certainly said something when he got up to speak, but it could hardly have been construed as the right thing. The food had not been that good and Williams told the assembled throng: 'The last time I had food like this I was in a Vietnamese camp'! That went down with more of a lump than the lousy food. There were all kinds of half-suppressed guffaws from the Wallabies, sniggers from others. From the heavies, there was the kind of silence you might expect from a headmaster just about to mete out punishment to an errant pupil. I don't think Steve Williams was made captain for a while after that!

Discipline was always strict on that tour, and it was a topic Jonesy used to preach constantly. But of course, as with all rugby touring parties, you always find the occasional example of rogue behaviour, however minor it might be in comparison with the activities of some rugby players from certain nations I could mention. For example, we were not in the same class as some notorious members of a British Lions touring party of recent years who made a pact that they would walk through doors which did not open, rather than open them first. As they were touring New Zealand, a country in which automatic doors were probably only introduced a few weeks ago, you can imagine the damage that was done.

When any of our guys did step out of line, however marginally, the 'judge' on hand to consider the case was someone I would like to have hear any case I might ever be involved in in real life. Dr Charles Wilson, 'Chilla' to one and all, was one of the greatest managers I have ever known on a tour. Chilla was a marvellous bloke and undoubtedly played a key role in the overall success of the trip. He would summon you to his room with the stern words: 'Right, you'd better come and see me at six o'clock, because you are in trouble'. When you got there, he'd say, 'Well, you'd better have a few drinks now you're here', and you would proceed to have a great old yarn about anything and everything except for the original reason you were there in the first place! And then he'd say, 'Right, don't do it again, and now off you go'. The courts of the world need Dr Charles Wilson to administer justice!

We certainly had plenty of laughs on that tour, as well as playing winning rugby. But then, that is the ideal combination for a successful tour. You get your work done, prepare conscientiously for every game or training session, but then have a good time together when you are free. I don't know whether you could call one incident after a match in Scotland a good time, but it was certainly some do. Cameron Lillicrap, our prop forward, had played his first game after a three-week lay-off through injury. That evening, Mark Ella and I went out for a few drinks or a meal or something, and just as we got back to our hotel, we noticed a cab pulling up outside the hotel. 'Crapper', as he was known to all and sundry, was in the back. I don't know why, or what happened, but Lillicrap went up to the driver's window to pay the fare and ended up throwing the money in the guy's face. That did it – an angry Australian against a volatile, incensed Glaswegian who immediately announced that he was going to call the police. Mark and I leaped into the debate and tried to persuade the bloke not to get the cops while Lillicrap was shouting at him, 'Come on, I'll fight you'. This was not quite what was called for in the circumstances.

Well, we eventually dragged Cameron inside the place, and quite soon he fell fast asleep on a pool table and was to be heard snoring his head off. This din was matched only by the sound, a few minutes later, of police sirens coming up the drive from everywhere. The taxi driver had been true to his word. It was at times like this that Alan Jones was so good. He solved the problem, as he always did. He preached loyalty to his players and he certainly proved the value of it by demonstrating that trait when it was needed. Wilson and Jones were an excellent management duo on that tour, a strong management which showed loyalty to its players but also came down hard on anyone who broke the rules. That was fair enough.

I am no patron saint of good behaviour, but equally, I have never had anything but contempt for people who go on tour and cause major damage. Activities such as turning on fire hoses, burning bedding and letting loose terrified animals in hotel dining-rooms might bring a smile to your face, but I don't think they're really too clever. I assume there is not much intelligence in guys who do such things because basically, you are condemning all your fellow rugby players around the world as a lot of overgrown schoolboys who cannot behave and don't know how to control themselves. I resent such a generalisation, but I am quite sure a lot of people who have seen such things do hand out such damning comments.

In my view, when you go on tour you are representing your country and people remember that, if and when there is trouble. Besides, no one needs to go over the top to have a good time. People are watching you, it is essential that you behave. But I believe too many British players hold the mistaken belief that they own the world and can do just what they like. Look at British soccer fans: they just destroy things when they go abroad and it must be because they think they are *it*. It happens with English cricket tours abroad, too. There was a shocking tour they made to New Zealand a few years ago; all sorts of stories came out about that and about the behaviour of certain individuals. These people are idiots because they let down their country. There is no need for any of it, and you certainly don't need people like that on rugby tours. Under Alan Jones, we enjoyed ourselves in 1984 but we knew about accepted standards of behaviour. Nor did it do any of us the slightest harm to be aware of those boundaries. For a start, everyone knows you, and you should try to establish a good reputation on and off the field. If you have to turn to alcohol and smash up people and property just to have a good time, you must be pretty sick in the head.

One of Alan Jones' achievements was to integrate a squad which, of necessity, contained players from the two states which fight each other like cat and dog: Queensland and New South Wales. On that 1984 tour, I was the only player in the entire party who came from the ACT, which meant that neither the Queenslanders nor the New South Wales guys showed any natural caution or suspicion towards me. But I found that all the peace and harmony vanished very quickly when I went up to Sydney to work and play my rugby a few years later. I was a New South Wales guy then, and attitudes changed almost overnight. To people outside Australia, it might seem hard to understand, but the rivalry between the two states has always been fierce. I guess it has deep historical origins and will always be that way. But my belief is that when you go away together to play for Australia, all that should be left firmly behind. Nothing should come between you when you represent the Wallabies, and in 1984, Jones made sure it didn't.

If you look at that tour in chronological order, you see that we didn't make the greatest start in the world. We beat London, as I have said, but then managed only a 12-12 draw with the English South-West Division. Worse still, we lost to Cardiff 16-12 four days later, but that defeat turned out to be the worst possible result, not for us but for the Welsh. They closed their eyes to the reality that the Australian team finished the match strongly. The inherent arrogance of the Welsh quickly emerged as we were written off as a thoroughly ordinary touring party. This played into the hands of a guy strong on psychology like Alan Jones.

We beat England in the first international, comfortably enough in the end (19-3), and then went to Ireland, where we won the Test 16-9. In those days, it was very unusual and difficult to play two countries in a single week. It demanded great concentration and commitment on the part of the players to regroup after England to meet Ireland, all within seven days. We led 6-0 and then trailed 6-9 as Ireland came back at us, but Mark Ella first dropped a goal to level the scores, and then supported me on the outside for the decisive try. 'Noddy' Lynagh added a goal to take us clear.

And so to Wales, which we knew would be probably the big one for us. If we won there, only Scotland would stand between us and a Grand Slam, and with all due respect to the Scots, we didn't see them as party-spoilers. But that was to get ahead of ourselves, and Jonesy never let us do that.

Of all the memories I have from that tour, perhaps the single most vivid one is of lying on my bed the night before the Welsh Test, having just got over a bout of 'flu, and watching the Welsh coach on television saying that Wales could beat Australia nine times out of ten. Well, you should never say that before a Test match, whoever you are playing. For a start, it's arrogant and rude to your visitors, and furthermore it's very unwise. It provides your opponents with all the motivation they need, and boy, did Jonesy milk that situation to the full! He came pounding out of his room as soon as the interview was over, stopping at each room to say, 'Can you believe the arrogance of these people? Just listen to what this guy said . . .'. I would say that by ten o'clock on that Friday night Australia had won the Test match at Cardiff the next day!

By the time we went out to face Wales the following afternoon, Alan Jones had been to every member of his team and asked him a question: 'Roger Gould, can your opponent beat you nine times out of ten?' 'David Campese, can your opponent beat you nine times out of ten?'. Every player roared out his answer. We were ready to eat Wales by the time we went out. We just knew we were going to flog them. By that time, anyway, we were becoming a very good team and hardly needed any extra motivation. But we got it, great bucketsfull, whether we needed it or not, and Wales never stood a chance.

Before the start, the dressing-room was, unusually, very, very quiet. But that was no problem; it showed how hard we were all concentrating on what we had to do. Then we went out and did it. We took Wales apart clinically and ruthlessly. It was the first time I had played at Cardiff, and what a souvenir it was to take away! But for people to reckon that Cardiff Arms Park is a holy ground I thought was a load of rubbish. To me, it was just another ground; why is that particular one so special?

An English friend of mine felt badly let down by our performance that day. He had invited his girlfriend down to Cardiff with him, telling her that she would not have lived until she'd had the hairs on the back of her neck raised by the sound of the Welsh singing at a Cardiff international. Halfway through the second half, when that great wall of sound normally rises up from the terracing, there was nothing but groans. And when our hooker, Tom Turtle – or Tommy Lawton as he is more properly known – called Samson at a scrum-five near the Welsh line, and the Wallaby pack heaved the Welsh forwards back over their own line so fast it was like a train going into sudden reverse, you could have heard a pin drop on that hallowed grass. In many ways, you can trace the shocking decline of Welsh rugby in recent years to that single incident from our 1984 tour. The blow we struck went to the very heart of Welsh rugby and its soul seems to have been mortally wounded ever since.

Of course, the Welsh coach should have kicked himself for a month afterwards: he was an absolute idiot. What you say to your team in the privacy of their own dressing-room is your affair, but if you ever want to make the opposition play well and beat you, then coming out with comments like that in public is the way to do it. Maybe the Welsh think they are supreme in rugby, but those days are gone. Obviously, Wales have been a great force at periodic stages of the game's history, but no longer, just as all nations experience a rise and fall in their fortunes. I think the problem that is peculiar to the Welsh is that they grow up with delusions of being the best . . . or at least, they have done until now.

That very night in Cardiff, only hours after we had flogged Wales 28-9, their players turned up at the after-match dinner and one of them, Robert Ackerman, said: 'You can't say your players are better individually than ours. Man on man, there is little difference'. As someone once said, you never beat the Welsh. It is just that sometimes you score more points than them.

I scoffed at the so-called mysticism of Cardiff and that was my sincere belief. For me, all these supposed shrines – Twickenham, Cardiff, Lansdowne Road, Murrayfield – are all just patches of grass. I found it strange that people talked about such places with so much awe. At least, that was my first impression on my initial visit to those grounds. But having played there a few times since, I now realise that without the great tradition of such grounds, rugby in Britain would not mean as much as it does. I'm sorry if I offended anybody with my first thoughts, but at least you have now had the considered opinion!

Edinburgh was to be the scene of our Grand Slam and we let no one down. Scotland 12, Australia 37 shouted the scoreboard at the end; four tries to nil in our favour was perhaps an even more relevant statistic. We had taken on the best of British rugby and shown them how to play the game properly, scoring 12 tries in just four Test matches. Our four opponents scored just one try between them, and that came right at the end from David Bishop for Wales at Cardiff when we already led 28-3. We deserved to complete that Grand Slam against Scotland because we did not take anything easily, or assume success. We never once relaxed. We went out and did a solid, professional job. No one thought it would be easy because Jones had got it into our minds that the guys we were playing were not turning up just to play the role of sacrificial lambs. So we gave them the respect the Welsh coach never gave us.

That day in Edinburgh we all played well. It was do or die, our chance to make the record books, so we were never going to let that opportunity slip away, especially not for so stupid a reason as being too casual and not preparing properly beforehand. Now, looking back, I don't believe many Australian sides will ever play like that again. It wasn't just the fact that we did it, it was the style in which we triumphed: what was it Jonesy kept on about? . . . to win without style is to triumph without glory. Well, we played with a lot of style that day; we were not cocky but we did play with enormous assurance. We all knew what to do and what we did, we did very well and most efficiently.

Looking back on that Grand Slam achievement, I have regrets that Australian rugby does not seem to have progressed from those heights, although of course in 1986 we did win the Bledisloe Cup in New Zealand. But those achievements aside, there has been a disturbing lack of clear direction in the Australian game at international level after the example we set, from which England, in particular, have obviously learned in subsequent years. Alas, we seem to have forgotten those important lessons. The old saying 'Practise what you preach' has slipped our memories. In no way would I want to diminish our achievement, but I have to be honest and say that I don't think the standard of British and Irish rugby was crash-hot at the time. I had read and heard so much about great British players of the past; men like Edwards and John, Duckham and Gibson, J.P.R. Williams and Ward, McBride, Wheeler and Cotton, to name but a few. But the flair demonstrated by most of those players seemed to have been lost to the British game, and that shocked and disappointed me. All they were doing was playing basic rugby and waiting for the goal-kickers to score points. And were they good at that!

We played 18 matches on that tour, and our opponents collectively booted a grand total of 46 penalty goals, while scoring between the lot of them a measly 11 tries (unless you count the final match, against the Barbarians, when five tries were run in against us in a frenzy of throw-it-around rugby). If that were not the ultimate indictment of British and Irish rugby and the stranglehold penalty kicking had on the game in that part of the world, then I don't know what would be. The Brits were kicking mad, even to the extent of trying to drop goals from the halfway line rather than attempting to score tries by moving the ball. It has always been my deepest belief that to win rugby games you must score tries. OK, it is good to win and useful to have a top-class goal-kicker. I must admit, too, that sometimes Australia have won, especially in recent years, only because of their goal-kicker, Michael Lynagh. But the way I want to play and the manner in which I seek to win is by scoring more tries than the opposition. Where is the pleasure for spectators in seeing a guy lining up penalty kicks all day? And do players enjoy standing around watching a mate booting for goal six or seven times? I can tell you I don't. Most teams have 15 players who all want to do something with the ball, to feel it through their hands and to try something entertaining when they have possession.

As a back, I am incensed if all I am asked to do is chase kicks ahead downfield. If I wanted to do a series of 100-metre sprints, I might just as well have a go at it in the Olympics. Besides, there is still a little more money in athletics than rugby! (Sorry, I was only joking . . .)

When we left Britain, we had set an example of how to play running rugby. Not *the* perfect, 100 per cent example – that probably doesn't exist. But we had demonstrated that it was perfectly possible to win and entertain at the same time. The challenge had been thrown down to the British and Irish nations, and so when the Wallabies went back to Britain, in 1988 for a short tour of England and Scotland, I was pleased to see that Scotland had improved a lot. So, too, had England, and these two countries seemed to be leading the way for the Home countries. The Scots and English seemed determined to run the ball at us and showed that they had learned things from the 1984 Australian tour. We beat both countries pretty easily in 1984, but four years later England beat us at Twickenham, 28-19, outscoring us in the try count by 4-3. Scotland managed two tries at Murrayfield, but we ran in five in a 32-13 win. By that stage of the tour our form had improved drastically from that shown in the English sector.

I thought the rugby in both countries was significantly better. Scotland's perennial problem is that they do not have enough people playing the game in their country. What they do achieve from such a small base of support is, in many respects, remarkable. They will, I imagine, always have difficulties but then so, too, will Ireland, if their decision to cap Brian Smith is any indication. That was an awful comment on their lack of home-grown talent. Even if Brian Smith was the best player in the world, how could he have been termed Irish? He has not lived in the country, which is a genuine qualification. Even he admitted when he was chosen for them for the first time that of course he was Australian, felt Australian and always would do. At least he was open and honest about it all.

My grandmother had some connections with Ireland, so presumably I could play for them. Someone else who certainly could is the New Zealand Maori breakaway flanker Eric Rush, with whom I played in the Barbarians side, in the 1990 English Barbarians' Centenary celebration games, against England and Wales. Rush is a super player, as fast as lightning, and what he would do for Irish rugby is incalculable. But is Eric really Irish? If he is, I'm an Eskimo! You begin to think that anyone whose grandmother once changed ships in Cork Harbour would be qualified to play for Ireland. As far as I am concerned, you play for your own country, unless you happen to be living on a long-term basis in another country. John Gallagher, an English-man who played for New Zealand because he lived there, is a good example. These short-term acquisitions are doing nothing to help solve a country's long-term problems. They might help win a few games, but it is a long-term supply of home-grown talent, springing up from a healthy domestic game, that every country seeks.

Wales are in a lot of trouble as the 1990s get underway, but I'm pleased to see that they have not been trawling for recruits in the South Pacific, even though the history books tell us that many Welsh settlers went out to Australasia in the 1800s. The problem facing Wales, dare I say it, seems to be a lack of pride in their national team. How else can you explain the sudden and now constant drain of resources to Rugby League clubs in the north of England? There was surely a time when Welsh players, seeing the current plight of their country's national side, would have laid down their lives to help improve things. The modern-day guys seem to be asking when the first train leaves for Widnes. They have lost a lot, but I imagine many more will go after the 1991 World Cup. Losing a player like Jonathan Davies was a huge blow. How can you fill a gap like that? The same problem afflicts us in Australia, for we lost five Test backs in two years to League. Nor will it stop there: how can you be a force in world rugby if you are losing players like that every year? It is impossible. Australia have done remarkably well to achieve what they have, given this constant haemorrhage of talent to League.

While we are on the subject of British teams, I'd like to say a few things about that most famous of all British clubs, the Barbarians. When I talked in the opening chapter about why I had rejected some pretty lucrative offers from Rugby League, I omitted to recount another factor: the point that League cannot offer you the kind of honour that is associated with playing for the Barbarians. That is special. I guess the Barbarians is the classic English gentlemen's sporting club. Yet I am convinced it still has a worthy, and indeed important, role to play in the future of the game. I know that the club traditionally chooses a player who is uncapped – Eric Rush, the New Zealand Maori who is not yet a full All Black, was the obvious example during the 1990 Centenary celebration matches against England and Wales.

But I believe that ethos should be greatly broadened to offer many future internationals their chance of making a mark in such company. This applies equally to the Australian Barbarians, the French Barbarians and all such associated teams.

By all means, if the Barbarians are facing a touring team, pick a strong forward pack, but then go for young, exciting backs to help them and give them a chance to become established. What does it matter if the Barbarians lose a match? After all, they are supposed to be in existence to help players have a good time and transmit that pleasure to the spectators. I suppose star names bring in more people through the gate, but there should be a balance. For example, I remember reading about the first time Denis Charvet, that thrilling French centre, played in some invitation match in England. He made a colossal impact; but before that game, he was unknown outside France. It is that kind of player the Barbarians ought to be looking to include in their games.

My advice to the Barbarians is be bolder in your team selections, look further than just the star names. If it means that players like myself do not get called up so often, then that's just tough stuff on us, much as we have enjoyed our times with the club. Every club should look to the future, which does not always mean looking back to past performers who have made their names. Putting up-and-coming stars into Barbarians games can give them the confidence they need to go on to develop their careers. They find out if they can handle that level.

The first time I encountered the British Barbarians was in 1984, when the Wallabies played them in the final match of our tour. We beat them 37-30 in a match which boasted 11 tries. My first appearance for them came at Leicester in a traditional fixture always played two days after Christmas, invariably before a sell-out crowd of 17,000. My fellow countrymen may have to look twice at this figure, given the fact that only 9,000 turned up to see the Sydney Grand Final at Concord Oval in 1990, between Randwick and Eastern Suburbs. For 17,000 people to see an invitation game every year bears testimony to the appeal of the Barbarians in English rugby.

Of course, being Brits, there are some funny old ways and even funnier old codgers associated with the Barbarians. I sense that a lot of Barbarians rugby is arranged for the old guys in the committee box. It offers them the opportunity to turn up and have a good time, to talk about when they used to play and generally to live happily in the past. It certainly surprised me to see so many veterans at the pre-match lunch and the dinner afterwards, sipping all the red wine and clutching their pint pots of beer. I thought it was supposed to be a players' game, and yet they invite you to play and you have to pay £4.00 ($10.00) to buy a tie! And it's the devil's own job trying to get a Barbarians jersey. I was lucky; Mickey Steele-Bodger gave me a tie, but that's not the way it is normally. Yet you are playing in front of 17,000 people at one match alone, and you honestly wonder where all the money goes.

The first time I went to that match at Leicester, I was in the restaurant or the lounge somewhere, and some old chap came up to me and announced in that rather grand English tone: 'I played, you know'. Whether this was designed to bring me to my knees in admiration I was not quite sure, but I wasn't about to be rude to the guy whatever he said. I don't believe in that. I said something to the effect that that must have been nice, and he went on, 'In fact, I probably played against your father'. Given that my father never played rugby, I somewhat doubt it. The memory of that meeting often brings a smile to my face but being civil to the guy didn't cost me anything. I just said 'Probably not'.

I am always amused by Brits like that. They seem to think you want to know all about their playing days. It's probably not fair to condemn the Barbarians on that evidence; it just amuses me to come across people like that. I couldn't really care whether the old chap, or I, for that matter, played against the King of Thailand! That is all gone, history now. All I am interested in is playing and enjoying matches. This, after all, is 1991 not 1961.

Another thing I found strange about the Barbarians was their selection policy. The first year I was invited to represent them against Leicester, we had three Frenchmen in our side and I found myself handling the ball all afternoon. Twelve months later, when I went back, there were none. Instead, we had a couple of English centres and I hardly touched the ball the whole match! We also had a Welsh five-eighth, Adrian Davies, who insisted on standing directly behind his half-back to take the scrum ball so that he found it virtually impossible even to get over the gain line. All very strange! The Barbarians are renowned for their running rugby but there wasn't much of it on display that second year at Leicester.

Another role I believe the Barbarians could fulfil is to take a tour to countries where rugby is not yet that big. I am thinking of places like the Netherlands, Spain, Romania, Italy, the USSR, Canada and the USA and perhaps some of the Pacific nations, especially Japan. They could take a few experienced players, that people would have heard of such as Will Carling, Gavin Hastings, Robert Jones, Donal Lenihan and Serge Blanco, but also, following that thought I had earlier, include plenty of up-and-coming youngsters yet to make their names on the world circuit, players who would benefit as young men not only from playing rugby alongside some world-class performers but also from the experience of touring and seeing places like Leningrad, Bucharest and Tokyo.

You could get the best players, the most experienced ones on the tour to conduct coaching clinics in these countries. I would love to go on something like that and help pass on whatever knowledge I have of the game to players from less developed rugby-playing countries. It would help those countries enormously, be valuable for the host players and most interesting for the Barbarians players, too. Just think about the potential for a Barbarians tour to the Pacific basin alone: Japan, Western Samoa, Tonga and Fiji. It would stimulate interest enormously in those countries. The combination of raising standards among the countries visited as well as giving your own emerging players great experience of rugby and life isn't a bad one. I don't believe I am the only senior international who would be more than delighted to go on such a tour.

Tradition is all right in its place but it should never be the sole reason for a club's existence. Everyone should look forward more than they look back, and the Barbarians could serve the game worldwide in a wonderful way if they undertook such a tour. I cannot believe they would not find enough sponsors, either, especially if they spent any time at all in a country like Japan.

CHAPTER
— 6 —

NEW ZEALAND

It has long seemed to me a very good idea that if ever I needed to take out a contract to kill someone, I should go not to a shady underworld figure in Australia but one of the 15 members of the New Zealand All Black rugby side! After all, they have been carrying out the merciless execution of rugby players and their hopes for years, and doing such a clean, clinical job that their professionalism has been acknowledged the world over.

Since I made my international Test debut against New Zealand in Christchurch on our 1982 tour, I have played the All Blacks 18 times in full Tests, and I have come out on the winning side in just five of those games. When you play the All Blacks, you are playing the best in the world. There can be no other plumb-line with which to gauge your own form. They set themselves the very highest standards of performance as a norm, and if you cannot aspire to those peaks yourselves as a team, then you are gone. There is simply no place for the weak-hearted, for those short on confidence or self-belief, when playing the All Blacks. Theirs is a history of ruthlessly crushing any inferior opposition, and you know the stakes when you go out to face them.

To win a Test match against New Zealand is to know a feeling of deep satisfaction and pleasure at the completion of a job thoroughly well done. There is no other sense of elation comparable that I know of in all inter-national sport – you cannot beat the All Blacks *without* playing efficiently and well. In all the years I have been playing the All Blacks, I can honestl say that I have never seen a bad New Zealand side. Of course, some were better than others, but you could not have looked back on one of them and said they were a bad side. There is an inherent ability in every New

Zealand rugby team that goes out on to the paddock, more so than any other rugby-playing nation on earth. Each and every team wearing the silver fern knows its task; it understands how much is expected of it, and it is formidably aware of the price of failure. That has been, and always will be, an enormous source of power and performance, for I don't believe there is a New Zealander born who does not understand all about the importance of the All Blacks doing well.

It is from this deep well of tradition, which has grown up over the last 100 years, that New Zealand's extraordinary success rate comes. To establish the sort of legend for which the All Blacks are now known takes time. A side must withstand close scrutiny of its record, it has to show its consistency and, above all else, it has to keep winning. Not every now and then, like most countries, but on a regular basis. And when it loses, there is such an outpouring of national grief and dismay that every member of that team, or the next one which goes out on to the field, must be left in not the slightest doubt that he is playing that day, not for himself or even just his mates, but for his whole country. That is how much winning rugby matches at Test level means to New Zealanders.

Wherever I go in the world, people often ask me just what it is that marks out the All Blacks as so special on the rugby field. There is an intrigue, a mysticism about them on which they trade cleverly. You won't come across a New Zealander rubbishing his own team; that is off limits. They build this well of inner belief which touches every fibre of the player going out to represent New Zealand in a Test match. Filled with that sense of history, destiny and importance, is it any wonder that these guys play a rugby match as though their very lives depended on it?

The All Blacks are so good for all these reasons and many more besides. There is an aura about playing for the All Blacks which is instilled at birth, and if the baby happens to be a girl, well, the child grows up just as desperate to represent New Zealand at hockey or netball. Just because you are talking about a girl in no way diminishes the burning ambition and desire to represent New Zealand; I'm willing to bet that any netball international would feel every bit as much pride and play with just as much passion and commitment as an All Black tight head or scrum-half.

This factor is explained by the country itself and its geographical location, or, more particularly, isolation. The place is a long way adrift of most of the rest of the world and therefore tends to look inwards as opposed to outwards. When it does that, it probably finds comparatively few fields in which it can rival the rest of the world. For example, New Zealand's industry or commerce would not be able to take on that of countries like the USA or Germany and come out on top, nor would it produce the number of historians associated with a country of centuries-old tradition such as

England. But one thing in which New Zealand can stand shoulder to shoulder with the rest of the world is rugby football, so the team which represents them at the sport carries not just the hopes of a few thousand individuals who happen to follow that particular sport but those of the entire nation.

I have toured New Zealand enough times to appreciate that the knowledge of ordinary men and women in the street about the All Blacks is quite astonishing. Most women can hold conversations with you about the merits of the pack chosen for the next All Blacks Test and whether so and so ought to be in ahead of someone else. The first time I encountered this, I was puzzled. Haven't even the women got anything better to occupy their minds than rugby, I thought to myself. But after I considered it for a while, I quickly realised why this was. Just as a European probably has a sizeable knowledge of history and especially recent wars in that part of the world such as the Second World War, which so ravaged the continent, and an American is well clued up on politics, which plays such a big part in that country, so a New Zealander, male or female, knows a lot about the thing for which the country is renowned. In this case, rugby football.

It is against this background of nationwide interest, that the All Blacks have established their invincibility. Plainly, they have had to, for failure would not have been accepted by a whole country. It would be like the USA suddenly finding itself unable to choose a president. When England lost the Grand Slam, Triple Crown and Five Nations Championship title to Scotland in a dramatic afternoon in Edinburgh in March 1990, I am willing to bet that literally millions of the English did not even know that a rugby match was taking place. Millions more may have done, but did not really care about the outcome. And still millions more might even have been interested enough to watch the match on television or read about it in the newspapers the next day, but then just shrugged and got on with their lives. Life goes on in London, I am quite sure, when England are playing an international at Twickenham, however important the game. People don't care; it is just another sports event.

Had the All Blacks, for example, lost the 1987 World Cup final to France in Auckland, I'm willing to bet the whole country would have been hushed in its dismay. National mourning might not have been officially declared but it would have existed in reality. There would not have been a soul in the country, whatever their sex, unaware of the All Blacks' defeat. In my experience, that is utterly unique in the world. As for the country I come from, such a scenario is laughable. You could ask half the jokers in King's Cross or Macquarie Street on the day of a Test match who the Wallabies were playing and they'd probably tell you they didn't even know the Wallabies *were* playing that day. I'm willing to bet that some of them wouldn't even know who the Wallabies were!

I guess when most of us play Test rugby we feel a particular pleasure for either ourselves, or our families, especially Mum and Dad, or our close friends, or a combination of them all. But it never struck me when I first wore the Wallaby shirt that my whole country was sitting on the edge of its seat, hanging on the result. I never had the feeling that people in the outback were crammed together in silence, listening to a broadcast of the match and praying that their boys would do the business! Australia is so vast a country that more than half of it has no interest whatsoever in rugby football. New Zealand's small size contributes to their sense of togetherness.

It is their attitude which marks these guys out as special. They hate losing. No one in the whole world hates losing as much as an All Black – he would lay down his life for a win. OK, I hate losing, too, and I feel lousy when it happens. But there are too many other things in my life and the life of my country for us to be downhearted for very long just because we lost a rugby match. Jokers get up the next morning and go surfing; others go off to the races; millions more are off partying or having barbies. A land as big and as varied as ours has too many things going on for a single rugby match to matter very much. I suppose the closest we ever come to this unique situation is when the Ashes are being fought for in cricket, because that is a sport played all over Australia whereas rugby football, Australian Rules and many others sports are only played in certain states. But even with cricket, if the team loses we tend to rubbish the lot of them and get on with our lives! There are still other things which matter far more to us, like whether the grog shop is open and how we can get a better deal at work so that we can work fewer hours for more money. Hang sport – those things are far more essential!

Australia is like paradise. It has everything in terms of climatic appeal, a good standard of living and a wide variety of sporting outlets. The sun shines in summer and winter; you can swim every day of the year in most places, and if you happen to live in the northern half of the country, it is like having summer 12 months of the year. New Zealand is different.

The weather is rarely very hot or sunny, and is usually cold and wet through the long winter months. The scenery is outstanding, and New Zealand remains one of the best countries in the world in that respect. If you have never been there, I'd urge you to go because the sight of the Southern Alps in wintertime, with a hard frost across the Canterbury plains and snow all over the mountains, is one of the great wonders of the world. As rugby players, we tend not to go to tourist centres such as Queenstown, but you can see the great New Zealand winter scenery from the window of your tour bus as you head for the next town.

Yet New Zealand can be pretty bleak, particularly in winter. The harsh cold, tough country breeds a tough character. Without doubt, New Zealanders are tougher as a people than Australians. If one guy's life involves getting up at 5.00 am on a freezing winter's morning to look after his animals out on the hills, while another's revolves around a gentle swim on the beach in the morning sunshine, then it doesn't take too much to work out that one guy has it a whole lot easier than the other. New Zealanders live in a beautiful but physically harsh, indeed cruel, country. Australia has its ruggedness but, generally speaking, the majority of the population does not live in these remote areas. The people congregate in and around the cities on the coast, and with the best will in the world and all due respect to Aussies, you couldn't say that living in Perth or Sydney was as tough as making a living out in the wilds of New Zealand's South Island.

To beat New Zealand at rugby takes a discipline, a dedication not required against any other country of the rugby-playing world. You need rigid concentration for every moment of the 80 minutes. Allow yourself the luxury of losing that peak of concentration for even a moment and you can bet that the All Blacks will take advantage of it. They are masters at sniffing out a weakness in the opposition and capitalising on it in an instant. They intimidate you just by their presence. There is something even about their name: when you tell people you are playing the All Blacks there is almost a hush of reverence and respect. It is as though everyone understands this as the ultimate challenge. You are attempting to knock the top bird off the perch. Of course, the All Black players themselves trade on this all the time. They are keener than anyone to extend the legend because it helps their cause no end. I don't think it is necessarily true of the Wallabies, because we play them so often, but a lot of teams are humbled even before they go out to meet New Zealand. It is as though they feel they have no right to be on the same field as the mighty All Blacks. This, it really goes without saying, is completely the wrong attitude to take on to the park against them. You have to build up a sense of invincibility among yourselves and believe you are better than them. An inferiority complex when you play the All Blacks is absolutely useless; you might as well not bother to even turn up.

The New Zealanders are an arrogant people when it comes to rugby at the top level, but I suppose they have plenty of reason to feel pretty smart. I just wish Australia had been half as successful in recent years. But, when it comes to the crunch, it simply does not mean quite as much to us. To New Zealanders, victory for the All Blacks means everything; more than anything else whatsoever in their whole lives. I don't believe any nation in the world can rival that intensity because it is freakish. Certainly the British and Irish people cannot match that desire; to them, it is jolly nice to do well and win, but it is only a part of their lives.

Because of this intensity, the New Zealanders often become blinded to reality and objectivity; plain common sense, if you like. When we beat them in Wellington in the final Test of our 1990 tour, having already lost the first two Tests and therefore the series, it brought to an end a phenomenal New Zealand victory march which went back 22 Test matches to 1986 and Nantes, where they lost to the French. In all, counting provincial games New Zealand had played on tours in that time, they had gone 50 games without a defeat. Unbelievable. And yet, that night in Wellington after our victory, I heard people saying that it should have been the end for the All Black coach, Alex Wyllie. He had failed; it was time for a change. That attitude is crazy, utterly ridiculous . . . and yet it is the reason the All Blacks stay on top of the pile in world rugby.

I respect New Zealanders deeply. I am treated extremely well when I go there. Generally speaking, there is much antipathy between Australians and New Zealanders, yet I get along well with them. Through our shared times in Italian rugby, I have got to know New Zealanders like John Kirwan, Craig Green, Mike Brewer and others. I enjoy their company and think they're great guys. And during that 1990 tour I got into some of the pubs and clubs of New Zealand and met ordinary Kiwis with whom I would probably never have rubbed shoulders had my sport not taken me into their midst. I enjoyed their company and had a great time with them.

I could not live in New Zealand, though; it is rather too quiet for my liking. And I would not want to live in a country where people lived just for rugby – it would drive me nuts. At least in Australia and Italy you can get away from rugby if you want to – people do think and talk about other things. I'm not sure a great many New Zealanders could talk about anything other than rugby even if they wanted to, which I am sure they wouldn't!

I toured New Zealand for the first time in 1981 with the ACT side, when I was just 18 years old. I had been home from that tour only six weeks before I went back again, this time with the Australian Under-21 team. On those first two tours, I was fascinated by it all. I had heard so much about New Zealand rugby; this was the place where rugby really had a name and reputation. I watched closely to see how the teams we met went about the game. They all seemed to have a natural idea of what they were trying to do, and they certainly knew how to win. It was quickly obvious that rugby was their life. I knew even then that I could not be like that simply because, as an Australian, I had been brought up differently. I wasn't born to play for the Wallabies, and I wouldn't have wanted to eat, sleep and drink the idea of one day playing for my national team. To me, such fanaticism isn't healthy. Australians, by and large, have an aptitude for the easy-going life. If we think we are doing well, we will stop training or at least ease off. We don't have the commitment or discipline which seems to be a natural part of every All Black rugby player. Australians want to have a good time and if they can win a few rugby games as well, then that's great. But for New Zealanders, having a good time doesn't come into it if they are already All Blacks. They have been chosen to do a specific job, and unless they do it and keep on doing it. they believe they have failed. And I doubt whether anyone could live with a guy who considered himself to have failed as an All Black. It almost amounts to national shame.

I don't think I am being rude in saying that without rugby, there wouldn't be much going for New Zealand, apart from that exceptional scenery. So it becomes essential for them as a people that the All Blacks continue to dominate the game worldwide and make headlines everywhere they go. In many parts of the world, especially the British Isles, people still frown when you use the word 'professional' in association with a Rugby Union team. But when I use it to describe the All Blacks, it is meant as nothing less than the supreme compliment. They have got their approach down to perfection and they play like a professional team. The world champions never have slack training sessions or anything unprofessional like that. They plan, they prepare, they talk among themselves and they practise and practise until they have got it right. And then they practise a whole lot more. As an Aussie, I can only stand back and admire that kind of dedication, discipline and determination and admit that you wouldn't find it at a Wallaby training session.

This ruthless concentration is achieved no matter where they play. The Australians, when they are at home, find many distractions from wives, girlfriends and friends in general, so much so that sometimes you wonder after losing a Test whether it has been partly because of the fact that you had so many distractions during your period of preparation. Certainly, Australia's record in international rugby during my time in the side, through most of the 1980s, is erratic. We have had our spells of success, but even in those times we have inexplicably lost games we assumed we were going to win.

New Zealanders do not seem to suffer from these lapses. They seem able to live with the enormous pressures involved in the expectations of their nation. Believe me, it is a whole lot harder to beat any side in international sport when everyone assumes you are bound to win. It takes a special discipline to be able to go out and perform at your peak all the time in those circumstances, and New Zealanders don't do it once or twice but every damned time they go out on to the rugby field.

When they are beaten, New Zealanders absolutely hate it. The stink of defeat seems to fill their nostrils; it enters every cell of their body and eats into them. They cannot stand the thought that they have been a member of a beaten All Black side. It is as though it will be a stain on them for the rest of their lives. And I think that is absolutely the right attitude to have if you want to reach the top in any sport. Defeat has to hurt so much that you will give everything you have to try to avoid it. In a sense, too, the All Blacks are a bit like the Welsh when you beat them. They will come up with all manner of excuses for it, but it is not in them to accept that their opponents were just better than them and beat them fairly and squarely.

I get along with most of the current All Blacks side and enjoy a chat with them when we meet. But one increasing tendency I do not like is the way they often snub young lads waiting for autographs. Personally, I never mind spending time with the kids because I feel you must have their interest and support. They represent the future of our game, and without their interest, where will rugby get support and enthusiasm in future years? But I don't think New Zealanders spend enough time on that side of it, and I don't like to see them pushing kids aside when all they want is autographs. No one, not even the most famous All Black of modern times, should feel himself above signing autographs for kids who ask politely. It should be done as a pleasure not grudgingly as some sort of perceived duty.

On our tour of New Zealand in 1990, I formed the impression that the standard of rugby in the country was not quite as high as in previous years. Their attitude was still the same, although some teams clearly wanted to run the ball – on previous tours the universal style had been kick, kick, kick. Some teams this time, such as North Auckland and Auckland, wanted to have a go with the ball in their hands. But before anyone jumps to the absurd conclusion that I am writing off or rubbishing any New Zealand teams, let me repeat that the standard in their country is never bad. It is either good or very good! In 1982, for example, Bay of Plenty flogged the touring Wallabies and they did the same to us in 1990. We also lost to Waikato in the 1990 tour, but maybe the reason for that lay within our own camp.

The Australian Rugby Union, in their infinite wisdom, had decided that we would spend a week in Queensland at training camp before we flew over to New Zealand to start our tour. This we did, training on hard grounds in warm sunshine, and then took the Tuesday afternoon flight across the Tasman, landing in Auckland. We went by bus down to Hamilton that night and then had to go out the next afternoon to play Waikato, the second toughest of all the New Zealand provincial teams at the time and, predictably, we lost. As a piece of planning wisdom, it was about as brilliant as making Concord Oval the venue for Test rugby in Sydney!

You just cannot take that kind of liberty with New Zealand teams. Touring there is no picnic, and to treat a major provincial side with the disdain that schedule implied was absurd. You expect a hard game whenever you play a match in New Zealand, whether it is against the All Blacks or a provincial side. The fact that we are Australians is reason alone for the locals to raise their game to unknown heights. It is a bit like waving a red flag in front of an enraged bull; you know they will come at you as hard as they can. Most New Zealand sides are well-drilled and what made our tour so especially difficult in 1990 was the fact that Scotland had just toured the country and emerged unbeaten against all the provincial sides. This was doubtless taken as a personal affront by every New Zealand provincial side and instantly doubled the difficulty we were likely to encounter at each game. Kiwis just love beating Aussies.

Scotland had lost both Tests against the All Blacks earlier in the season but the second, in Auckland, had been close: the Blacks just sneaked home by 21-18. Perhaps that persuaded people that, in the light of our Test series win over the French, we were favourites. Whoever made public that sentiment did us scant favour. We were lulled into a false sense of security and yet, on the day, we were also intimidated because we didn't play our natural game, preferring instead to sit back and wait for them to come at us. Also, we didn't kick well that day, particularly Michael Lynagh. I hardly saw the ball, and when I did I was clobbered. Not feeling the ball in my hands destroys me anyway; I cannot take it. That day, we were more afraid of making a mistake, worrying about who we were playing against, rather than getting on with our own game. And when we did run it we were totally predictable. The Blacks knew the ball would head out to me when it was shifted, and so whenever I got it they hammered me.

New Zealand won all the good ball going that day and even the fact that Grant Fox missed about five kicks at goal didn't really matter. It was the old story: the All Blacks were vastly superior and our blasé attitude was blown apart. Perhaps we even thought we were going to win, but you can never have that attitude against New Zealand. To beat them, you must go out and concentrate completely on your own game with no expectations what-soever of victory, and just keep concentrating on doing the basics correctly. Then, maybe, just maybe, you will find yourself in with a chance of winning. And you have to grab that chance with both hands, because as sure as day follows night, it won't come around again for some time.

By the second Test at Eden Park, Auckland, we had improved a lot. It was a Test match we could have won, rather than should have won. Had our wing from Randwick, John Flett, touched the ball down when he reached the New Zealand line, we could have made 20-17 with the kick to come – considering we had come back from the dead, we were on a roll. But John lost the ball over the line and our hopes disappeared with that lost, bouncing ball. The Blacks, typically, made good their fortune by getting down to the other end and scoring the points which made sure they clinched not only the Test but also the series. Another series against New

Zealand had gone west; we were plunged into the ultimate depression.

We knew we could have played better in that Test. The fact that we had got so close to the Blacks proved we were close to them in ability, and when it came to the third Test in Wellington, we had a sense of giving everything to salvage our reputation. New Zealand had not won a Test match against Australia in Wellington since 1982. Not so long ago, you might think, but let me tell you, that is a lifetime by New Zealand's standards. And what happened that day really angered me. We played as though our lives depended on it; we tackled them as though they were demons; we knocked them back and we kept at them, mercilessly hounding them when they had possession and flattening them in some shuddering tackles. Not surprisingly, it won us the Test, but immediately apparent was the question: why the hell hadn't we played like that in the first two Tests?

This All Black side had not been, in my estimation, as good as the one we had come up against in 1982 on my first tour over there. Yet there were still some superb performers. Mike Brewer, for example, had a lot of stick in his own country, but I would have no hesitation in naming him one of the world's greatest back row players. He is a real unsung hero of New Zealand rugby, in my book. Zinzan Brooke also played well against us, whatever his problems on the tour of France which followed our series against New Zealand that year.

New Zealand have 15 outstanding individuals in their side but perhaps Grant Fox is the key to the team. It will be mighty interesting to see what happens when Fox retires, because without him, perhaps they would not have won as many games as they have done in recent years. His partner against us, Graeme Bachop, is not to my mind one of the great New Zealand scrum-halves. He might be an efficient link in the unit, but you cannot rate him among the all-time best All Black half-backs such as Dave Loveridge, David Kirk and Sid Going.

The only successful way to play New Zealand is to meet them head-on, put them down on the floor in the tackle and stop them getting any of their famous forward rolls going. They do not really have that many established moves; probably no more than seven in total. But unless you keep tackling them and preventing that momentum, they need only employ two or three set moves, and those are enough to win most games. What they do, or what they are allowed to do, they do extremely well. That is the bottom line when you face the All Blacks. But push them back behind the advantage line and suddenly they look mortal. Then, but only then, you are on the way to beating them, because they cannot go anywhere against consistently heavy tackling.

In 1986, when we won the series in New Zealand 2-1 under Alan Jones, we had the discipline, the self-belief and the personnel to do the job. Also, we did the work required and, perhaps most important of all, we *wanted* to win. Four years later, I don't think we were really determined enough to win. We didn't work hard enough to beat them and we didn't spend sufficient time ironing out the little individual faults in our own games, which we had done in 1986. I found that even when we had not trained very well on a particular day, we just finished the session and packed up. That would never have happened in 1986: we would have kept at it until it was right. We did not have as good an atmosphere within the team. Even some of the experienced guys in 1990 did not seem to want to be as close a part of the team as everyone had been determined to be in 1986.

I'll give you an example. We had 5,000 T-shirts printed to sell during the tour, the profits going to the players' tour fund. Some of us took the trouble to go out, put ourselves about and sell those T-shirts so that there would be a decent kitty to share out by the end of the tour. Peter FitzSimons, our lock forward, was especially good at this – he even wore a T-shirt to a team dinner in Dunedin. He got plenty of stick for that from certain other members of the touring squad, but Fitzie's only intent was to spread the message about selling the T-shirts. Others were nowhere near as good at doing their bit, but mind you, they were not slow in coming forward for their share of the spoils when it came to handing out some cash at the end of the tour. To me, that was an indication of the fact that not everyone on this tour was prepared to integrate and do their bit for their mates. They didn't want to enter into the spirit of the thing. If you do not have a real team, in the true sense of the word, off the field then how are you going to have one on the field?

I really thought on that tour that the attitude of some players when they were not selected for the Test team showed that being dropped did not really matter enough to them. It was as though playing for Australia was not everything to them, which it should have been. It was certainly a very different attitude to that shown in previous years. I imagine that had such an attitude surfaced in the New Zealand squad, the 'elders' within the All Blacks, the senior, established players, would have cut it out like a surgeon wielding the scalpel on a rogue growth. That is why the Blacks always do so well on the field; they have 15 players willing to give everything for their country and their team-mates.

On our tour of 1986 everyone in New Zealand hated us, as far as we could tell. But then, we went over there and won the Test series. Four years later, it seemed equally clear that the New Zealanders liked us immensely – but we ended up losing the series! It depends what you want when you go to New Zealand: 1982 was different, we were not expected to win a single game because we were such a young team. The fact that we not only won several provincial matches but also took a Test off the All Blacks, doing so with a brand of exciting, entertaining rugby which had a real zip to it, made us even more popular. But when it comes down to winning a series over there, you have to be deadly serious, full of intent and determined to take no shit whatsoever from your opponents. You also have to be prepared to stand together, give your last breath for the cause and shirk nothing in terms of commitment.

In 1986 we fulfilled those criteria in every way. In 1990, we failed the test, in more ways than one. And, as with any side facing the All Blacks with flaws in its make-up, we were exposed and then beaten.

CHAPTER
— 7 —

SPEEDING TO DISASTER: THE LIONS TOUR OF 1989

My preparations for the tour of Australia by the 1989 British Lions were conducted in the world of the Pyramids, bustling Arab street markets and camels! Once the Italian championship had ended, without success for Milan, I stopped off in Egypt on the journey home to recharge the batteries and feel some warm sunshine on my back once again.

The only problem with being a 12-month-a-year rugby player is that you end up going from winter to winter. The international cricketer has it made on that front. So, as a small consolation, I laid up, rested and relaxed under a warm Egyptian sun for ten days. I suppose by the standards of the locals it was not that hot. The temperature had probably crashed down to around only 31 degrees (88 degrees Fahrenheit) but I lapped it up. I still trained; not by running along any of those bustling Cairo streets where the motor car fumes rise into the air like a plague of attacking bees, but by running along the beaches. At night, when the temperature had cooled, I would do some sprint work on the beach.

I stayed at a Red Sea resort, about an hour and a half out of Cairo by plane. It was a long way away and very quiet. Monica, who had heard all about it, came with me. We didn't do many tourist-type things – I was there chiefly to enjoy the sun and relax, and I did that all right. I'm perfectly happy lazing around on a beach in the sunshine (find me an Aussie who isn't and I'll find you a nice, quiet, traffic-free street in Cairo!).

By the time I had negotiated the perils of Cairo Airport and crossed the world to reach Sydney, the Lions were in the country and starting to stage something of a mopping-up job on the outposts of the game in our country. Beginning a rugby tour of Australia with a match in Perth against Western

Australia might make geographical sense, but at best it could only be compared with taking a high ball on the rugby field with half-a-dozen six-year-olds trying to outjump you for it! That's no disrespect to the Perth locals, but the Lions' first two games, in Perth and Melbourne, were really only excuses to spread out the tour around the country so that the visitors saw something of Australia apart from New South Wales and Queensland.

It always seemed fairly clear that the opposition presented by Queensland at Ballymore for the Lions' third match would be their first decent examination, and so it proved. It turned out to be the usual old British rugby stuff; the Lions won because they kicked their goals. Oh, and they scored a try, which was something Queensland couldn't manage in the entire 80 minutes! From afar, it looked like ideal stuff to turn on at one in the morning when you couldn't quite get to sleep. Lynagh kicked five penalty goals for Queensland, Gavin Hastings replied with three, and Chalmers dropped two goals for the Lions. Stalemate – apart from the fact that Robert Jones did something very odd indeed in the context of that match: he scored a try. The Lions won 19-15 but the New South Wales boys who saw it were by no means scared by the evidence before them.

New South Wales met the Lions in the fifth match of the tour, and the idea was for us to move the ball. However, our first problem was in winning it in the first place from the line-outs because Ackford, the English lock, had a very good game indeed and kept our possession in that phase down to a minimum. We did score a good try through Roebuck, who converted it himself and also kicked five penalty goals. There were several times when we might have gone on to score other tries, but we could not finish off positions which looked promising. And once again, I thought there was too much kicking from the home side. In my opinion, New South Wales could have picked a better five-eighth who had more experience of international rugby. Instead, we played Kent Bray, who I thought made a few bad decisions that day.

The Lions got away with it, beating us 23-21 with Chalmers again dropping crucial goals, three in all. But it seemed to me an odd way of going through a tour. I thought the Lions' backs looked very ordinary against us, hopeless even; the only reason the tourists had beaten both Queensland and New South Wales was because their forwards had done a very efficient job indeed. When Ackford came out to Australia he was not well known, but those Wallabies who had been to England and Scotland the previous year had seen him in action – he made his Test debut against us at Twickenham at the ripe old age of 30 years 9 months! You can't accuse the Poms of rushing players into international rugby before they are ready for it, can you?

Ackford was one of several big, heavy forwards the Lions selected for their team for the first Test at the Sydney Football Stadium. Thankfully, common sense had at last prevailed among the Australian Rugby Union and the authorities had bitten the bullet and turned away from Concord Oval, that unloved, unlovely ground out in the western suburbs of the city. How anyone conceived that place as the future home of Australian international rugby is beyond belief; always *was* beyond the belief of the players. We told the relevant people in authority as much at the time the whole crazy project was being considered, but of course, those people never listen to the players, what do they know? They only play the game. So millions of dollars were invested in Concord and millions of dollars were washed down the drains of that part of the city. The whole thing was a disaster from start to finish and a shocking indictment of the stubbornness and intransigence of people in authority. They had made up their own minds and they were determined to go ahead with the plans no matter what the uproar or disapproval over them. They knew best, those people always do. And the New South Wales Rugby Union is still today bearing a financial burden which will cripple them for years to come.

Concord was not only miles away from anywhere, it was not even in an area which had the character and appeal of Paddington, which is close to the old Sydney Cricket Ground where the rugby Tests used to be played. Paddington is filled with pubs and clubs, and whenever a major Test match is played in Sydney you will find thousands of fans inside the pubs and restaurants, before and after the game, having a beer with their mates or a meal later that evening. It is a bit like Richmond and Twickenham. Richmond is the place to head for after a Twickenham international: it has some great pubs and eating houses and is nearby.

By contrast, Concord was never going to make it as a venue for international rugby, compared with the SCG or, when that was no longer available, the Sydney Football Stadium. Two crowds tell the story. For the 1987 World Cup quarter-final between Australia and Ireland at Concord, around 17,500 people turned up: for the first Test against the British Lions two years later there was a sell-out 40,000 crowd. Explain that, if you want to defend Concord: nobody can – Concord is and was always going to be a graveyard for international rugby. Thank God it has been consigned to the backwaters, to be used only for minor games. It was a pity we had to have the 1990 Grand Final staged there: it would have been so much better at the SFS.

On the field, one thing about Australian rugby was worrying me increasingly. The tactics we were employing more and more were, in my view, a desertion of the traditional Australian game of flowing back-line play. The trend could be traced back to the latter years of the Alan Jones era, particularly the 1987 World Cup. Our tactics there were to get the ball down to the opposition's half and to try for some penalties to get points on the board. Then, if we got into a fairly comfortable position on the score-board and we were in the right part of the pitch, we could start running it. You had to go back to 1984 and our tour of the UK to find some decent running rugby, especially from deeper positions.

Of course, in 1984 we had had the best of both worlds. We'd had Lynagh outside Ella, the latter being a player who fancied running, and the former a player who had been brought up in the school of safety first through kicking. This was the ideal balance, because if we had to kick, Lynagh was there. It was a tragedy for Australian rugby that this perfect blend ended so early with the retirement of Ella. I do not believe Australian back play has ever been as penetrative since Ella retired. People know he is a friend of mine and will doubtless accuse me of being biased, but the facts support my argument. There was in 1984 a movement, a desire to run which was never as convincing after Ella finished.

We missed from Ella the natural lead in the way to play that kind of game. I do not dispute the argument that Michael Lynagh is a fine player, of course he is. But the first option of all the Queensland five-eighths has always been to kick. That is the way they have been brought up. Mark Ella's first movement and thought was not to kick; his idea was to run and, if need be, transfer the pressure by giving it to the second five-eighth (inside centre) or to take it up himself. A good example of how much easier it is to play against the first five-eighth who relies basically on kicking was seen in 1986 in the second Test of our tour of New Zealand. At Dunedin that day, all the New Zealand flanker Jock Hobbs did was to run at Lynagh, and Noddy just didn't know what to do. He put up bombs but they were not spot-on because he was under such pressure. And that was not good enough.

I accept that, especially in Test matches, there will be times when you have to kick. I am not a complete idiot, a total romantic fool who does not recognise that fact and wants only to run the ball all the time from every position. Besides, the surprise element which I believe is so valuable to the side attacking from deep in its own territory would be completely lost if every ball were run. But in an increasing number of games nowadays forwards are dominating matches and behind them, their first five-eighth is kicking the leather off the ball. That's an ugly sight in a game which can produce some highly attractive play, and the trend disturbs me.

Nor, I can tell you, do the All Blacks follow such a blinkered policy. They have a guy in their team called John Kirwan and they make damned sure they give him the ball because they know what he can do. Those who condemn the All Blacks as a kicking machine under Grant Fox don't watch rugby closely enough. They have scored some superb tries since Fox has been in the side because Grant is a player who can and does spread the play as well as keeping it tight when necessary.

When you look at the old video tapes, you see players like Gerald Davies, J.J. Williams and Michael O'Connor running the ball whenever and wherever they could. And frequently they succeeded gloriously, often against expectation, but always with the conviction that theirs was the approach to follow, the creed to take up. They failed sometimes and certainly conceded some tries in those moments. But I am willing to bet they came out on top many more times than they failed, and you would have thought the game would have learned from such people and their exciting philosophies. But nowadays the game has become so much more technical and tactical. There are unwritten laws which cramp the game: don't get caught in your own half, don't try to run it, don't open out until you are near the opposition's 22, don't risk it, it's not worth it. I just don't buy all that garbage, and it's obvious that the All Blacks agree with me. You only have to watch them to see that.

What all this means is that the game has changed, and for the worse. There have been times recently when I have felt that the standard in Australian rugby was very poor. Not only were individual skills inferior, but teams did not seem to have any style about them. Maybe I am guilty of expecting too much, but is it a crime to want to see fast, open rugby played in the way for which the game is supposed to have been invented? My fear is that we have moved a long way away from that, and for the life of me I fail to see why. The enterprising game, based on attack and flair, is so much more enjoyable for players and spectators. Who really wants the drab, forward-dominated, sterile, penalty-kicking rubbish that is seen time and time again today? And if, at the end of such a match, a team comes out just ahead of another, so what? Which side can honestly say they have achieved anything? The winners of such a contest are kidding themselves. They have achieved nothing at all except to undermine the very future of the game they supposedly like so much.

Does anybody in the United Kingdom, for example, ask themselves why Wales have lost so many players to Rugby League in recent years? Sure, money is a major factor. But look at Wales' miserable record and miserable rugby of recent times. Would so many have gone to Rugby League if Wales were playing fast, open, attractive and positive rugby in which the backs had a real chance to run with the ball and to see what damage they could do? I doubt it. It seems to me that the players who have been faced with that decision have probably decided that they had nothing to lose by turning professional. Rugby has itself to blame if that is true in even one case. Rugby around the world has changed. There has been a new revolution. It is now only about winning; winning at all costs. If you have to stand on a guy's head to win, then do so. If you have to kick six penalty goals to win, then kick them, and then go out and celebrate, even if the other side has scored four tries to your none.

The philosophy these days is don't do anything spectacular. Bring in 40,000 or 60,000 people, but don't entertain them, kick the ball all day. Anything you like, but just win. That, it is said, will be enough for them and for you. Bullshit. It is fraudulent really: it doesn't make full use of guys like me who can be versatile. We are regarded as people to be left out on the sidelines, just given the ball two or three times to see what might happen. We are a sort of old-fashioned curiosity, to be indulged in once or twice in 80 minutes, but never to be considered as potentially crucial match-winning factors. I can tell you this: it is like being left on a mantelpiece and being brought down from time to time. I feel increasingly like a curious old relic in the boring games which dominate far too often these days. I guess I am always liable to be criticised because of the way I play. Mine is a high-risk game, and I am bound to make errors. And I have to accept the flak when it does fly, because I am the kind of player who can lose as well as win a game. It's great when it goes well, but you're the chief clown if you have loused it up. You get all sorts of stick then. At least I am prepared to have a go, to put my head on the block, but rugby generally at the moment is far too cautious, it's all safety first.

In Australia, in 1990, it was said that the young Queensland centres, Jason Little and Tim Horan, were the best in all of Australia. Yet in a Queensland-New South Wales game that year, I swear those two guys could not have had the ball in their hands moving forward down the line more than twice in the entire match. How can they be called the best centres in Australia when they are not being allowed to demonstrate their running talents? Players have changed, skills have changed and the mentality has changed. Winning is very important, I am the first to concede that, and not every single match is going to be a delight either to watch or to play in, but the majority ought to be occasions for pleasure. Sadly, that is all too rarely the reality. At times in the last couple of years, I confess I have not enjoyed my rugby at all. I have felt that I have been wasting my time, apart from when I played for Randwick, where the attitude never changes. It made me feel like going straight back to Italy, because at least I'd had some fun over there. I began to feel like an outcast in senior Australian rugby.

The 1989 Lions series was the first staged at the Sydney Football Stadium. When we met the Lions in the first Test on 1 July, we knew they had several big forwards, so we thought we would try to move them around the paddock to see how quickly they would cover the ground. The answer was pretty slowly. Jeff Miller won a lot of ball on the ground, Scott Gourlay rampaged around the place, and although the ball rarely got out as far as me on the wing, I could see that we were adopting some pretty sensible tactics and that they were working well. Michael Lynagh kicked the goals when he had the chance, but no one could say we relied on penalties to win. We outscored the Lions by four tries to nil, and our win, 30-12 from a half-time lead of 15-6, was conclusive. There were not many whingeing Poms around that afternoon.

The plan to make the Lions pack turn around and run back involved a lot of kicking from Lynagh, but it worked well that day because the tactics were extremely well executed. Not many of our blokes were concerned about anything that night: we had walloped the Brits by 30 points, and to win the first game of a three-match Test series puts you in pole position, the inside lane and everywhere else combined for the rest of the series. The idea of not going on to complete the task seemed impossible at that stage.

There were seven days between the first and second Tests, yet they seemed like seven years given the differing performances of the two sides on the day of the Brisbane Test. Ballymore was full for a game in which Australians confidently expected to complete the demolition of the Brits – we were one up in a three-Test series; it was there for the taking. But one thing probably nagged away at the back of our minds. Australian rugby has always had a problem stringing together two or three consecutive wins.

If you go back through the sporting history books, you will see this problem repeated time and again. Just about the only time we ever laid that bogey was in 1984, when we won the Grand Slam in the UK with four straight Test wins. Disregarding France whom we beat well in Sydney in 1986, the next time we had tough opposition was against the All Blacks on our 1986 tour of New Zealand. We won the first Test, and then what happened – we lost the second. We did win the third Test that time to take the series, but it had been a similar story in Australia in 1984. We beat New Zealand in the first Test of their tour, messed up the second and lost that, and finally went down in the third Test. Ridiculous. I couldn't tell you why this happens so often to Wallaby sides.

Even so, we had reason to believe we could finish off the Lions at Ballymore. They had been outplayed in Sydney – we had been yards faster and altogether more determined. That Australian side played like it wanted the victory more than anything else in the whole world – and we got it. By contrast, the second Test was a disaster for us. We still led the Lions 12-9 with under five minutes remaining, but we had been badly put off our game. The Lions had done that, plainly and simply, by intimidating us. They belted us and took us on physically, mostly in illegal ways. It wasn't far removed from blatant cheating: at best, it was a cynical manipulation of the supposed fair play tactics the Brits like to tell you the game they play is all about.

Robert Jones stood on Nick Farr-Jones' foot at a scrum, ever so calmly and deliberately; they had patently set out to distract us from playing rugby. Obviously, they thought they couldn't beat us by playing rugby alone so they tried something else, some dubious, dirty tactics. Because that is what they were. The Welsh half-back didn't leave it at standing on Nick's foot. He then twisted his studs into it, and all you see in the reruns is Nick suddenly lashing out. But watch the video closely, frame by frame, if you want to see the truth.

Our guys were taken out off the ball in the line-outs and obstructed in all kinds of other situations. It was all blatant intimidation and a poor comment on how far some coaches and players will go just to get a win at the end of a match. Hell, if it's that important to them, let's not bother to go on the field at all; let them have their win if they need it that badly. It was a shocking episode in the history of British rugby, and no one in the UK should have been proud of that team. They cheated their way to victory after a first Test which proved they were an inferior side to us.

Our problem was that we had no player to fill the role of what you might call an enforcer, a player the others would follow naturally; a leader, someone prepared to compete if the nonsense started. We became fragmented and the Lions knew it. We had made the crass mistake of believing that we were going out to engage in a game of football. By means of the Jones assault on our half-back and countless other incidents, the Lions hoped to put us off our game. And it worked, I suppose, if you regard such tactics as worthy of an international side. Later in the game, the Welsh prop Young kicked one of our players in the head. All sorts of things were happening because the Lions had got us in a fury with their tactics. They weren't subtle but they proved effective, I am sorry to say. Everyone in our side was incensed, including me.

The Lions didn't have much style, apart from when Gavin Hastings scored his try near the end. By then, under all the belting and intimidation we had taken, we had been knocked out of our concentration, and not surprisingly. We forgot to run the ball and to move the Lions pack around again; we kicked it, and not always very well. My feeling was that if we had really run the ball at them we would have buried them. But we were sucked into the battle they went out looking for, and we paid the penalty. We lost the Test in the last five minutes by 19-12. Our old bogey of failing to land successive Test wins had struck again.

If, like all my mates in the side, I felt that was a bad day, the one I was to have back in Sydney seven days later was a whole lot worse. That Test created a memory of me which I suppose some people will retain to their dying day. We pulled the Lions back to 9-9 with an Ian Williams try, but I suppose the game turned on two incidents. The first came when we had a scrum almost on the Lions' line. It was a fantastic position for a scoring opportunity, but the Lions won a tight head and escaped. I don't mind accepting my responsibility for the pass which ultimately cost us the game, but other things were just as important in different ways, like that lost tight head. We lost a lot of scrums that day because we could not control the ball properly. I believe that, man for man, we were the better rugby team, but the crucial problem was that we just did not know how to handle the situation. We couldn't take the pressure.

I suppose I should go through my feelings about *that* pass, which cost us the crucial try touched down by Ieuan Evans. I had made a similar move in the first half, which had worked, but on that occasion I had run the ball out myself without worrying about releasing anyone else. That is what I invariably do in that position if I am attempting to run – I put the onus on myself to make the attack work, rather than seeking help from other quarters. If you need that much help, you probably shouldn't be running from deep in the first place. But this time, when Andrew missed a dropped goal, I was immediately aware that Greg Martin was loose outside me. I was thinking of where he was and wasn't watching Evans' position. It was my fault because I tried to step inside and pass at once, thinking that Evans would come with me. In fact, when I passed, he was in between me and Martin, and when I threw such a hopeless pass he had a simple job in touching it down for the score.

What was in my mind, what had I really intended to do at that moment? I have to say that I don't really know. I think I should have gone myself because it was certainly a position to exploit. There was space and time to get out from our line and attack hard, perhaps as far as halfway or even further. But I felt sure that Evans would come with me to leave Martin a free run outside me. I suppose, subconsciously, I didn't attack the situation as hard or as directly as I would have done had I been alone.

Of course, the outcome would not have been so dire had my pass been respectable, but it was hardly the world's greatest by any stretch of the imagination. The ball caught Martin on the shoulder, I think, and Evans fell on it over the line. There was no way Martin was to blame; it was completely my fault. The orthodox thing to do would have been to belt the ball into touch, of course, but then orthodox methods have never appealed to me very much. Besides, any normal player could have done that. I still believe the idea was perfectly sound; it was just that the execution went wrong.

Perhaps I should qualify that remark about it being completely my fault because, with hindsight, I am not altogether certain that it was. Sure, the actual pass was a poor one, but if you really want to understand what was going through my mind at that stage, you have to look not at that isolated moment but at the entire game. It was another tight match, full of kicking and set-phase play. We didn't seem able or willing to open up the game and my role, as has so often been the case in recent times, was really just one of an onlooker. In such circumstances, I honestly wonder what I am doing out there, standing around getting cold. If any side wants to see the best of me, then they have to give me the ball. Without it, I'm like Fred Astaire without his shoes. I crave the ball in my hands, especially early on, just like so many leading goalkeepers from the world of soccer. They say that early touch settles them down, gives them confidence, and that they feel they are in the game. It is the same for me. If I go 20 minutes with hardly a touch, I don't feel I am part of the game. And that is what happened in Sydney that day.

Consequently, when I did get hold of the ball, my craving to do something with it overtook the logic of safety first. To me, in that situation, it made no difference whether it was a Test match or a Randwick club game; I just wanted to make a positive move with the ball in my hands, to get into the game and show my worth. If you have a wing who can be creative and score or make tries for others but hardly ever touches the ball, you might as well not choose him in the first place. You might as well pick a great brute who can just knock people down when they come near him, not someone able to fashion tries with the ball in his hand and some space in which to move.

Most people don't understand me, especially those among the general rugby following. If you want an ordinary wing, that's fine, but don't look up record books which tell you some players can score 30 or 40 Test tries in their career, and then wonder why your guys don't do that. So many players in Test rugby sit out on the wing and just wait for the ball to come to them. If it never arrives, they just don't do anything in that particular match. Someone who used to be guilty of this was the England wing Rory Underwood. How many matches must he have gone through without contributing a thing? Underwood has changed in recent times and does now look for the ball, which I believe all modern-day wings must do. They must also look for every possible attacking position, not just pose a threat when their centre releases them 30 yards from the line with only the full-back to beat. That is the easy part – it is when he is near his own 22, isolated and expected to kick for touch, that you find out whether a wing is different. If people think the fact that I have scored more Test tries than anyone else in history is worthwhile, then they have to accept the other side of me. It's known as taking the rough with the smooth.

Other sports demonstrate this point equally well. If a snooker player is kept away from the table for long periods he loses his touch. Easily pottable reds suddenly start to bounce back off the corner cushions; his fine-tuning, worked out in regular sessions at the table, has gone wrong through the inactivity. It is the same for me. I detest the kind of inactivity which frustrates so many wings in the modern-day game. It drives me nuts hanging around watching a colleague belting the ball off the park when I could be running it. The game is supposed to be about a bloke who picked up the ball and ran, or so I thought. His feat seems to have been consigned to the Dark Ages as far as most players these days are concerned. And the rubbish rugby which is produced as a result of this policy ought to be condemned. Most of it isn't worth crossing the street to see, let alone paying good money to watch.

The rest of that third Test against the Lions was about Australia trying to catch up. Some time late in the game I was held in a tackle. Play moved on and Australia was on the attack, 22 metres out from the Lions' try-line. David Sole, the Scottish prop, tackled me when I was still on my feet. As I attempted to follow the play, Sole would not let me go and, unfortunately, I tried to wriggle free and kicked him in the head. We were losing and I was angry and frustrated, especially after my mistake. It was a spur-of-the-moment response of which I am not proud. I will always remember it as a very poor action on my part, but I don't feel I have a reputation to be ashamed of. Ask anyone in the world whether Campo is a dirty player: they would laugh at the suggestion.

We were 19-12 down but closed the gap to 19-18 with two more penalties from Lynagh. In all, nine penalty goals were kicked in the match; five by Gavin Hastings, four by Lynagh. But we couldn't add the final score which would have clinched it. The Lions had won the Test and the series. I've never seen so many guys so depressed as afterwards in our dressing-room. They were not very happy at all with me. They didn't have to say anything; I knew it from the look in their eyes and the glances which came across the dressing-room at me, like arrows from a bow. I knew what they were thinking.

What hurt me the most that day was the fact that not a single player crossed that dressing-room floor to offer me a word of consolation. We all knew that words were useless, but some bland remark such as , 'Mate, don't worry about it, we all make mistakes' or 'Campo, it's one of those things; that's life' would have meant more than anything in the world to me. But no one came near me, and I was really disappointed with that. I was the black sheep, and weren't they letting me know what they thought, just by staying away from me. I felt let down. If it had happened to someone else, I swear I'd have said something to the guy, like 'Don't worry about it'. You know he will worry, for weeks to come, but at least it's a gesture. Australia is supposed to be strong on that 'mate' syndrome – it's a place where you stick by your mates in times of strife, or so they tell you. You could have fooled me that day.

Only one person fronted up to me in those awful moments of total exhaustion, self-recrimination and disappointment in the dressing-room beneath the Sydney Football Stadium. And that man must have been more disappointed than almost anyone else in the whole country at the loss of a Test series which was ours for the taking. Way back in 1982, I had been highly impressed with Bob Dwyer's work and help when I was a kid on the Wallaby tour of New Zealand. Dwyer was a brick then, and he was proving himself as a man again this time. He came over as I sat slumped in the dressing-room, put a hand on my shoulder and quietly spoke the sentence I'd hoped to hear from my team-mates: 'Mate, forget it. It's one of those things'. No one will ever know how much that meant to me then, and still does to this day.

It goes without saying, of course, that nothing and no one can console you in that situation. I went to the after-match reception, hung around there for 20 minutes or so and then just went home. I guess the car was being driven on auto-pilot; my mind was anywhere but in that car, thinking about everything except the road. Speed was irrelevant; I just wanted to put as much distance as possible between myself and that football stadium. I cleared the inner city area and reached the 60 kmh section a little further out into the suburbs. At that moment, Rob Andrew lined up the dropped goal, but the ball flew away to the right of the posts . . . I was past a slow-moving car . . . and on to the loose ball. I looked ahead up the road and saw little traffic . . . there seemed little defence as far as the halfway line. I put my foot down on the accelerator . . . and the surge of momentum in my body as I collected the ball and started to run it out of defence gave me a feeling of exhilaration. And then, disaster: I threw the pass, the ball went loose, Evans fell on it and the Lions had scored . . . and a blue flashing light dragged me back to the reality of driving home.

'Mate, do you know what speed you were doing in that 60 kmh section?' asked the police officer, peering in through the car's side window, like a potholer looking for an exit from some cave. He took in the car's interior and saw I was alone. I'd been that way for a punishing hour and a half. 'We tracked you at 104.'

I smiled and said: 'Mate, you're lucky you didn't catch me ten minutes earlier. I was doing 130 then!' That joke collapsed like an All Black forward through a rotten floorboard. I was booked. Perhaps the cop had been watching the rugby that afternoon!

When I did finally get home, I closed the door on the world. The Queen of England wouldn't have had a price on entry had she knocked at the door. I had a few drinks with Daryl and Julie, and that was it.

I can honestly say that even six months after that match, some Australian journalists who used to call me at all hours of the day and night when it suited them had still not spoken to me. Not that I was heartbroken at that state of affairs, but it brought home to me the way some of those guys react. I thoroughly appreciated the few calls I did have, from friends telling me it wasn't the end of the world. It might have felt like it that Saturday night but it wasn't. The journos had a field day at my expense, and the inquest seemed to drag on for weeks. OK, blame someone for a major mistake like that – I accept criticism if it is justified, and it certainly was in that case. But for a whole week? I hadn't broken into anyone's house and assaulted the children; I hadn't mugged the city's Mayor and I hadn't got hold of a computer and hacked into a bank's security system to pilfer millions of bucks. But if you'd dragged a stranger into town and asked him about it, he'd probably have thought I was a modern-day Ned Kelly, guilty of the most appalling crimes known to mankind. You honestly wonder at the perspective of some of these people.

The criticism didn't only come from authentic journos. Former players, some of them old team-mates of mine like Andrew Slack up in Brisbane, started leaping into print about what a mess I'd made of things and why I'd done it. My rugby in Italy was dragged into it and blamed – ridiculous! For one mistake? When I played alongside Slacky I thought he was a great guy, but I have to say that the scenario in which a former mate can take you to the cleaners in the papers just because he's joined the journos' ranks isn't the most appealing to me. I suspect it wouldn't appeal to a great many other players, either. I hope I never get myself into a position where I start publicly slagging off guys I have just finished playing alongside. To me, there is something basically wrong with that. As I said, what the hell happened to the notion of old mates sticking together? No one can seriously expect to play international rugby and not pick up criticism from time to time, but some of the flak I took over that bad pass was way over the top, Kalashnikov stuff.

A similar situation arose in Lille in 1989, against France, when Australia was attacking. Greg Martin received the ball and threw a pass towards Jason Little, but the French centre, Andrieu, intercepted the pass and ran 65 metres to score. Strangely, Andrew Slack, once again in the Australian paper, said that it was not Martin's fault: it was uncharacteristic of him, a player who had worked so hard to get where he was. You could not blame him, said Slacky. Not bad from a Queenslander about a Queenslander. But that's Queensland for you . . . amazing, isn't it?

At the end of that series against the Lions, I knew that we could and should have won it, despite my pass. So did Bob Dwyer and my team-mates. The Lions won chiefly by figuring out where they could beat us, but I honestly think we lost the series more than they won it. Any side which was one up in a three-Test series and ahead with five minutes left in the second Test would inevitably feel that way. The Lions did well enough in the end, but I really don't think they were the world's greatest team. They had some good backs but didn't use them much; generally, it was safety-first rugby. All they really did was kick the ball up in the air or down the touchline and let the forwards advance. OK, they ran it off fourth- or fifth-phase, but any lousy team can do that; it is easy then. We didn't help our cause – we played into their hands by kicking too much ball away.

When the Lions headed for home, I was pretty glad to see the back of them. Their presence and the memories they left were too painful for me to think about.

CHAPTER
— 8 —

THE LONER

If the general public perception of an international rugby player is one of a hugely confident personality, holding court to 20 or 30 strangers for hours on end in a rugby clubhouse and putting down ten pints of beer in an evening, then I have to tell you that I don't fit the bill. I'm a loner.

You could mistake me for the local vicar's son, I'm so quiet! The only time I go out on the town is when I go on tour with the guys. Then, after games, or perhaps during the week, and when you are in another country, it is good fun being with your mates. But in Australia, you would have about as much chance of spotting a platypus without its bill as seeing yours truly out living it up for a night . . . unless it's Grand Final night in Sydney, of course.

I like to be by myself. After matches, I go to the Randwick clubhouse for 20 minutes or so, but then I head for home. I might pick up a pizza on the way and sit at home, either on my own or with Daryl and Julie. I have become increasingly used to my own company since I started going to live and play in Italy for six to eight months of the year. I am not sure my team-mates always understand that – rugby is supposed to be very strong on mateyness. My preference for solitude is not a sign of arrogance or aloofness, it is just the way I am. Nowadays, most of the guys in the Australian team have either wives or long-standing girlfriends with whom they spend a lot of time when we are in Australia. That situation is all right for a while, but I am not keen on the idea of a woman coming into my life and telling me how to lead it.

In most cases, someone in a relationship, especially one which has been going on for some time, wants to take an increasing amount of the other's time or space. At this stage of my life, I do not want that. Rugby has all my commitment at the moment, and there are still a few goals I want to achieve. I find it necessary to be alone to concentrate totally in order to do this. I thought that Monica, my ex-girlfriend in Italy, was the right lady for me. But after we had known each other for 12 months, she began to ask questions like, 'Do you have to go and play in this match?', 'Why do you want to go there?' and 'What are you doing that for?'. I couldn't handle that. I said, 'Hold on, this is my rugby life and I regard it as sacred'. I have worked so hard to get where I am now that I don't want anyone questioning why I am going to a particular match and whether it is really that important. That is not right. This factor had a lot to do with why we ultimately broke up.

Perhaps only an exceptional person can understand the need of another to be alone at times. If I were going out with someone well-known in sport, I would say, 'OK, do it, I won't disturb you', because I would understand what that person had to go through. And I would feel that if the relationship was really going to mean something on a long-term basis, then once the other person had completed what they wanted to do in sport, she would come back and perhaps the two of us would get together. I would not interfere in someone else's ambitions. But then, I have had the advantage of knowing what it is like to be dedicated to a sport, virtually to the exclusion of all other interests. I guess the person outside that world has not.

Things came to a head between Monica and I one Christmas after I had been invited to play for the Barbarians at Leicester. I found myself being questioned as to whether it was really necessary. That was too much; the split soon followed, for I could not understand why she should have said that. You can only play rugby for a certain length of time. Once you finish, that is it; you can never go back to it later in life. So while I am still playing I would like to do whatever I can and play wherever I can without having to justify that to anyone. I suppose I began to feel encircled, trapped if you like. After a while, too, you tend to fall into a certain pattern, and for me it is very hard to remain in that kind of orthodox situation. I have to break out and do my own thing.

I would love to find someone who would understand me. I am sure such women do exist. A guy I know sometimes just goes off on his own abroad for a short holiday, leaving his wife and children at home. He enjoys his own company occasionally and sees no need to justify his wish to go alone. His wife understands both him and the need for time to breathe in the relationship. That sounds ideal to me, but I don't think you come across too many women in the world who would be content with that arrangement. One woman who is like that is the wife of the former Ireland and British Lions

player Willie John McBride. After McBride had finished a long and distin-
guished playing career, he was invited to return to New Zealand in 1983 as
manager of the British Lions. An interviewer asked his wife what she
thought of the prospect of 'yer man' being away for another 14-week tour.
'That's all right,' she said, 'you can't live happily with a man who has not
achieved all he seeks'. What foresight.

In many ways, I am probably a very demanding person because I want
to do what I want to do so often. There is a tendency not to think too much
about the other person's wishes. But I suspect I am by no means the only
sportsman or sportswoman in the world who is like this. It may be because,
to reach the top in your sport, it is necessary not to let anything stand
between you and the fulfilment of your ambitions. It is a thread of selfish-
ness, but it is essential if you are to succeed in your chosen field. You feel
threatened if someone does come between you and your target because
they are undermining all that you have been striving for over many years.

Of course I get lonely – that is why I live with Daryl and Julie. I would
rather stay at home with them and have a nice conversation and a good
bottle of wine than go out and watch the guys drinking, or find myself in a
situation where I am chatting up girls I know I am highly unlikely to be
interested in by the end of the evening. To me, that is a waste of time. I
hate propping up bars and chatting idly without any purpose to the
conversation. Watching others drink a lot is not very pleasurable, either,
because I drink so little, if at all. I can't handle the sight of others getting
steadily influenced by alcohol. It bores me. I have a few drinks on special
occasions like the Rothmans Awards night. I have a good time in my own
way, but I don't like going overboard.

I believe that if you are a well-known figure – in sport, politics or
anything else – you have a duty to protect your public image. One of the
things I like about rugby is the fact that most people associated with the
game do have manners. You reach a stage where you have a reputation and
you want to maintain it. A player like Simon Poidevin has always understood
this and it is one of the reasons he is universally popular within the game.

If someone comes up to talk, you cannot say 'Get lost', or 'Leave me
alone' – well, I suppose you could, and doubtless some do. But I listen – no,
not all the time! – I haven't got the guts to tell someone to clear off. I would
never be involved in an all-in brawl, for example, because I am not the kind
of person to do that. You should have respect for people and show some
courtesy, even to the older ones who might go on a bit about their thoughts.
You have to understand that people want to talk to you because you are in
the limelight. On the 1990 tour of New Zealand I was working for Steinlager
(a company which is associated with Pepsi-7-Up). Part of my work commitments was to attend functions at the local pubs for an hour or so, just to talk

to the general public and to listen to their thoughts about the game. I really enjoyed this – it is one part of rugby I think all players should see. You get a totally different impression of the people and the country if you are on your own at these functions, especially in New Zealand.

I imagine for some guys, like Rugby League's Wally Lewis, it can become very wearisome, but I see it as my duty as a leading sportsman to spare some time for others. You find yourself talking to a wide variety of people. At the club at Randwick, for instance, I might have a six-year-old staring up at me, seeking an autograph, or a 66-year-old telling me what I did wrong in the match that day! I can handle that. Besides, if you listen, you might learn something. The perfect rugby player does not exist, so it is always valuable to listen to other people's views and opinions. Some of those old guys have been watching rugby for 40 years – they could probably teach the journos a few things, too!

It is all part of the game's fabric, meeting and perhaps having a drink with people you would otherwise not have met. Randwick, which has such a great tradition, is particularly good in this respect, but while it is important for players to behave responsibly and to demonstrate manners, I think it works two ways. Strangers should always remember too that the players will want some time with their team-mates, their wives and girlfriends or just on their own. What I cannot stand is guys who are half-drunk coming up to you and making a nuisance of themselves. In that state, they just impose themselves on the conversation. They are boring, often disgusting and a damned nuisance. I don't wish to spend any time with people in that condition. If they want to get drunk, that is their choice, but they have no right to barge into someone else's conversation and start throwing their views around.

I was in a bar in Sydney a few years ago with Nick Farr-Jones when a guy walked up to us and said something like, 'How are you, fellows?' Then he said, 'I won't disturb you, I'll leave you in peace'. Unfortunately, that was not the end of the story. About an hour later, after he'd had five or six beers, he returned with a few of his friends and decided to explain to Nick and myself about the time he broke his nose and the injuries he'd had. After what seemed an age, he said, 'You must really get hacked off with people like us annoying you all the time'. 'Yes', I said, and expressed my feelings in a few choice words. He still didn't understand. Eventually, Nick and I got up and walked out.

One of the guys I most admire in international sport is Ivan Lendl. I think he is a great tennis player, and I am also interested in the way he trains. But if I saw the guy in a bar or restaurant with some friends, I would never go up to him and start pestering him. The trouble is that everyone asks the same questions – how was the last tour, are we going to win the next match etc. etc. – and it all becomes a bit predictable. However, you take the good with the bad in any walk of life, and for all the people who do not have very many original ideas to convey, or are a bit the worse for drink, you meet others who are genuinely interesting and pleasant to talk to. I would never want to be cut off from the public, but I wish all people could be courteous. Some just want to be rude. After a Randwick match at Warringah a season or two back I was walking out of the bar and a guy said: 'Mate, don't play next week like you did today'. What can you say to that? I just bit my tongue and kept walking.

One of the things I do enjoy when I am in Sydney is a round of golf with Daryl early on a Sunday morning. I try to be on the course by 8.30 am, which is another reason why I am quite happy to rest at home on Saturday evenings and go to bed early. When you are training twice a week with Randwick, with a 45-minute drive across the city to get to Coogee and a similar journey home afterwards, and then training on your own on the other days of the week, you feel physically very tired. Although some people have the idea that leading sportsmen burn the candle at both ends, I don't think the successful ones do it very often. The average international rugby player is too concerned about maintaining his high levels of fitness and energy to spend hours in nightclubs.

While I do not doubt that some people in the game will not like to hear this, I have to say that it is not usually the public who expect too much of you but the authorities within the game. Their demands have become almost overbearing at times in recent years. To call Rugby Union an amateur sport is now so far removed from the truth as to be ridiculous. The idea of amateurism is that you can decide for yourself how much commitment you are prepared to make, how many times a week you want to go training and whether you want to play in a big club match or keep that longstanding promise to a friend to attend a wedding. But these decisions are increasingly being taken out of the hands of the so-called amateur rugby player.

Those who seek to excel at the game, to reach the highest level, in other words international rugby, are simply being informed that if they do not do certain things then they have no hope of being selected for their national team. It borders on blackmail really – do what we say, follow our programme and play in the matches we want to see you in, or you won't be considered for selection. And if some guy organising an event in Bermuda or Singapore or some such place calls you up and asks you to come over and play in his event, all expenses paid, you have to go to your union, if you live in certain countries, and ask them if you might be allowed to accept. And in a great many cases, they say no and you are left in a quandary – go ahead and damn them, or risk losing your chance of playing more international football. The situation is unbelievable in a sport which is supposed to epitomise free speech, free choice and general tolerance and understanding. It seems to me that the authorities these days do not just want their cake, they want to scoff the whole lot themselves, too.

Having made that point, I think the player himself has to be fair. I don't agree with players who inform selectors that they are available for the national team but not provincial sides. That is picking and choosing, and it's unfair to your team-mates and the selectors.

Please don't talk to me about greedy players. We are not in the same class as the administrators who think they have the right to keep the players down while they live it up in style, enjoying all the benefits of the players' talents without giving any recognition whatsoever to those who bring in the big crowds and the big-money sponsorship deals for the unions . You are just told when to turn up and that's it. If some players around the world, having watched all this happening over a period of time, have made their own arrangements to take some kind of financial advantage out of the game while they can, then I say good luck to them. You won't find me ratting on them.

Money-making bodies such as the national unions of each country are fighting hell-for-leather for as big a slice of the advertising cake as they can grab, yet until the last few months, if the players even whispered about the possibility of earning a few quid from speaking at a dinner or advertising a drink in their home town, the authorities would squash them from on high. Rugby Union has smacked of double standards for more years than I can remember and the main culprits have been the people in charge. Others would have better documentation than me on some of these things, but was it not an official of the English Rugby Union who, after a tour of South Africa a few years ago, suddenly had to give back certain valuable gifts which had been presented to him or his wife, when it became known what the gifts had actually been?

I'll give you another example of the way these jokers are not exactly backward in coming forward. During our 1989 tour to France, we visited the factory of the sports goods manufacturer Adidas, principally because they sponsored our boots. With the players on that visit came three officials from the Australian Rugby Union. As players, we wear track-suits, shorts, T-shirts and all kinds of sports gear almost every day of our lives, so it was interesting to see all this smart new gear laid out. But it seemed we were by no means the only ones with keen eyes. The players were each given a free pair of boots and the opportunity to buy whatever else we wanted at cost price. A few guys chose some stuff and paid for it, and we were just about ready to go when we became aware that the officials who were with us were by no means ready to leave; they had not yet collected their 'freebies' and there was no way they were going until they had them.

Someone once coined a phrase (it was probably Alan Jones – he always had the best phrases going) about the unpleasant sight of some players with their eyes out on stalks looking at the financial benefits available to them from the game. Well, I have to say, Jonesy, you never saw anything like this spectacle at the Adidas factory. Officials of a Rugby Union body hanging about with their hands outstretched, waiting for their freebies. It was a sight for sore eyes, all right, mate!

Earlier that year, the ARU had decided to arrange a new sponsorship deal, not with Adidas, but with Canterbury, the New Zealand sports manufacturing firm. Previously Adidas had sponsored all our kit; jerseys, shorts, track-suits and boots. Although they continued to sponsor our boots, the rest of the gear was acquired under a new sponsorship from Canterbury. Yet this in no way deterred the officials from hanging around for whatever they could get. I suppose it is the same as the process which leads to a decision on the venue for a future Olympic Games: the delegates probably need second homes in which to cram all the freebies they have collected by the time they have toured the world being wined, dined and fêted by representatives of the candidate cities, all of whom of course generously hand out any kind of gift they can think of to sway someone's vote. And to think some misguided people delude themselves that the Olympics is still the bastion of the amateur ethos! Come to think of it, I've heard rugby called the last bastion of amateurism.

When on earth will the game be honest and open with itself and face the reality of the situation? Who can honestly advocate going on with this hear no evil, see no evil sort of nonsense? Why doesn't the game wake up and start to behave as though it is part of the real world, rather than some throwback to Victorian times?

If you accused us, the players, of wanting a slice of the action, you would be met with a straight answer: yes – and why not? The authorities in Rugby Union care passionately about money, to the exclusion of a great many other aspects of the game. Those who administer the game would uphold the position taken by the Canterbury clothing company after they had asked me, through the ARU, to model some of their new range about 12 months ago.

Canterbury had done a deal with the Australian Rugby Union and wanted one of the players to model for a photo session. Whoever had posed for the pictures – Nick Farr-Jones, Michael Lynagh or Tim Gavin – the photographs would have gone around the world. The unspoken message would be that Michael Lynagh was recommending these clothes to the punter in the street. Come and look as smart as this; come and buy the gear.

I told the ARU that I would be perfectly willing to advertise the

COLORSPORT

COLORSPORT

COLORSPORT

Three of the leading coaches of my era. *Above left:* Alan Jones, who paid me the ultimate compliment for an Australian sportsman when he described me as 'the Bradman of rugby'. *Above right:* Jacques Fouroux, whose resignation as French national coach surprised me – I believe he would have cemented French rugby as a credible force for the World Cup. *Below:* Bob Dwyer, who has perhaps been pressurised since his reinstatement as Australian coach into changing his previously carefree philosophy.

A sea of faces and a sea of mud. *Above:* The Australian squad and friends celebrate our 1988 victory in the Cathay Pacific Hong Kong Sevens. *Below:* Rugby is not always glamorous! The 1983 event provided some of the worst conditions I've known.

Two of the great full-backs: Serge Blanco of France *(above)* and Roger Gould of Australia *(below)*.

Our captain Andrew Slack hoists the Bledisloe Cup after Australia's 2-1 series victory over New Zealand in 1986.

Influential All Blacks. I rate Mike Brewer *(above)* a top-class flanker. Grant Fox *(below)* has done much more for New Zealand in recent years than simply kick goals.

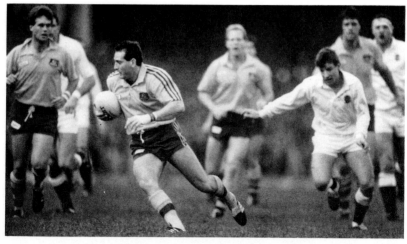

After Alan Jones's departure, I was determined to show that I could still play outstanding rugby. The 1988 tour to England and Scotland *(above)* gave me the chance.

An awful moment which I shall never forget: Ieuan Evans is about to touch down my wayward pass ... for the try that was to prove so costly in the Test series with the Lions in 1989.

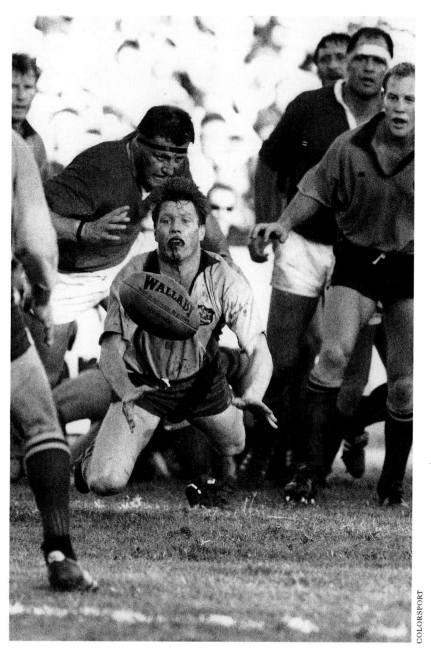

COLORSPORT

Nick Farr-Jones shows the battle scars of an increasingly antagonistic series in the second Test against the British Lions in Brisbane in 1989.

The All Blacks fail to score in the third Test of Australia's 1990 tour, a match we won 21-9.

Canterbury range in return for some financial remuneration. It was not going to be enough to outbid Kerry Packer for the latest mansion on the real estate market at Double Bay, but it might fund a visit to a decent store for a jacket or two. I think a sum of $1500 was mentioned. This suggestion was greeted stonily, to say the least. I could imagine how double agents whose cover had been broken were welcomed into the KGB's Moscow head-quarters in the old days of Cold War politics. True, I did not feel the cold metal of a pistol in the back of my neck before entering another world, but I saw the door soon enough. It was mentioned that a professional model would have cost them at least 5,000 bucks to hire for the photo session, perhaps a lot more, and that this wasn't a bad way of saying 'Thanks, mate' for all the efforts made on behalf of the ARU over the years. It wasn't as if any money would have come out of the ARU's coffers; Canterbury would have footed the bill. But nothing was forthcoming, and frankly, I didn't expect it. I know where these jokers stand and it's not on my side.

So what happened? Did Canterbury go ahead and hire a professional model to do the job and pay him the fee? Did they hell. They just used some old picture of me and did the promotion without even asking me. They don't care, they do what they want.

I didn't get a cent for that and I didn't get a cent for another ad I spotted in an English rugby magazine in 1990. I happened to be passing through London and picked up a copy just to look at it. On one of the pages was a big picture of me with my arms spread out wide, looking down, and right in front of me, superimposed on the photograph, was a bottle of a leading brand of bourbon. I couldn't believe it. There was some competition attached to it, but that didn't give anyone the right to plaster my picture all over a page which had a strong link to an alcoholic product. No permission had been sought and I would never have known about it had I not chanced upon the magazine. I was surprised to see, a year later in the same magazine, the same liquor company running another competition, this time using a picture of Will Carling. I am sure that Will was just as incensed as I was, and I'm just as sure he didn't get anything out of it either!

It is this exploitation of players that I find so appalling in modern-day rugby. People have been telling the players for more years than you can remember that they must never sell themselves because of their fame through the game. That learned body of men who form the International Rugby Board decided at their meeting in Edinburgh in 1990 that even though they were making what they called major concessions to the players, no one would be allowed to advertise or promote any products associated with the game. So Will Carling in England cannot advertise or recommend a particular make of boot and I cannot promote a certain company's rugby shirts. Yet the authorities will continue to enjoy an open field in making whatever deals they want with companies that have a direct link with rugby. It stinks really, doesn't it?

The IRB, in their infinite wisdom, even decided that players could not charge a fee for speaking at a rugby club dinner, unless that player's own national union gave general approval. This will doubtless mean that some unions won't care less and will allow the practice while others will strictly forbid it. Is that fair?

I am not against helping my national union in the promotion of the game. In fact, sometimes I wish they would use some of the well-known players a hell of a lot more to spread the message. But I do believe that the ARU and other unions throughout the world have to realise that they cannot take, take, take all the time. They have to give something back at some stage to the players, the ones who make it all possible for them, whether it is financial reward at the time or help with tickets when a Test match comes around. The situation at the moment is very nice for them but not much fun for the players.

I mentioned the Canterbury clothing company a little earlier, and I have to say that I don't think much of that company's policy at all. The final match the 1989 British Lions played on their tour of Australia was against an Anzac XV at Brisbane. Before the match even started, you could see that half the guys in the crowd were wearing the same jerseys as the players. To me, that cheapened and devalued the new jersey, as does any copy of a national team's jersey which is on general sale.

Of course, that is how they make their money, for there is an increasing demand for such jerseys for people to wear as leisure gear. But may I please be permitted to say that it does lessen the players' pleasure in wearing a special jersey. When the ARU had a deal with Adidas, the Australian Wallabies wore a super jersey which wasn't available in the shops. That is how it should be. If you gave one of those jerseys to a close friend it really meant something, precisely because it wasn't one that half the people in the room were likely to be wearing.

In 1986 when we toured New Zealand, Steinlager, the lager company which sponsored the series, gave the players some smart woollen sweaters with the teams' crest embossed on them. They were not overdone; just neat and classy. And they were for the players – you did not walk down Auckland's main shopping street and see half-a-dozen guys wearing them. It used to be a privilege to have an Australian jersey, but now every joker down the street has one somewhere in his locker. That is wrong, but the reason for it is simple – the desire of the authorities to make every last cent out of the game. They just grab the biggest financial deal going without any thought for the consequences.

I find it sad that all this nonsense goes on in a game in which it is still perfectly possible to find men of judgment, honesty, principle and sympathy for players. It is a fantastic sport for meeting people and making friends in all parts of the world. What has led to the great muddle and the double standards within the game is the failure of those in authority to chart a realistic path for the future of the sport and those in it. They have failed to adapt to contemporary society and have not understood that values which applied 100 years ago, however commendable they may have been then, may no longer be applicable as we move towards the year 2000.

Is there any harm in a commercial company using the players and giving them the same amount of money they would normally spend on promotions with anyone else? Why should players like Michael Lynagh, Nick Farr-Jones and me have to turn down these approaches; why should we not have been able to benefit when our services had been requested?

Sensitive would hardly be the first adjective to leap to mind when considering national selectors or administrators. For example, I resent the fact that when I return home from Italy at the start of an Australian season I have to prove myself all over again. Naas Botha, the South African, said much the same thing a while ago. Selectors seem to want to look at you to see if you are suddenly a bad player. But how can that be right when you have played something like 50 Test matches for the Wallabies? Why is it you constantly have to prove yourself? I would have thought a national coach should have been on good enough terms with his senior players to be able to call them up and say, 'How is your form, mate?', and enquire whether the guy is ready for Test match rugby. If the player is carrying an injury and is right out of form but tells the coach he's 100 per cent, then he is a fool to himself. But I don't believe that happens.

In 1990 I was dropped from an Australian Test side for the first time since my debut for the Wallabies in New Zealand on the 1982 tour. It was not a pleasant experience. What hurt me was two things: the fact that I was omitted because I did not return early enough from Italy and therefore (according to the word from on high) they could not assess my form in a club match, and the fact that I heard the news first on television. I did not agree with their decision then and I maintain to this day it was wrong. For a start, no one had telephoned me in Italy to tell me that they wanted me to go home early enough to fit in a game in which I could be watched and assessed. So I was suddenly left out, yet they know what I can do. They know I always give 100 per cent when I play in a Test match; they know I won't play if I am injured and they know me well enough, surely, to give me a ring to ask me directly whether I could handle a Test match so soon after coming home. Believe me, if I didn't think I could, I'd tell them so; there is no way I would go on to the paddock to make a fool of myself and let down my mates.

Having to prove yourself constantly is like a nagging headache which is always there worrying you. It creates a hell of a lot of unnecessary, additional pressure which you can frankly do without. While it is right that no one gets a free ride into the Wallaby Test side, surely the very senior guys merit some sort of leeway when it comes to applying basic rules? I mean, do people think it is all right to ask Nick Farr-Jones at the start of every season if he can still pass a ball off either hand? And is Michael Lynagh going to have to go through an examination with the selectors present to see if he can still find touch 50 metres downfield with a swirling wind? It's a nonsense and an insult to ask such things.

Hearing about your exclusion from a Test side from the television announcer, or from some journo who rings you up and wants a quote, isn't awfully nice. You have played 48 or 50 times for the Wallabies yet you are not even worth a 20 cent phone call from someone to say thanks for all you've done, mate, but on this occasion we're going with so and so. It would cost virtually nothing but it would mean so much. It is really no more than a courtesy. They would be putting you in the picture, taking the trouble to inform you and for that you would be grateful. Instead, after giving so much to rugby, you then have to suffer the humiliation of hearing the news second-hand. In any sport, that cannot be right. I think such treatment is disgraceful. Is it any wonder so many people on the administrative and official side of the game are viewed with deep suspicion or, worse still, contempt, by the players?

To me, comradeship and friendship come first in rugby, even before playing. The friends you have made through the game last for the rest of your life, certainly long after you've finished the playing side of the game. Those two qualities epitomise rugby football: they go a very long way to explain why some people turn their backs on the professional code, and why the friendships forged between people who have met through the game continue long, long after everyone has forgotten the result of any particular match.

During the 1990 French tour of Australia, I formed the opinion that the French understood this point better than the Australians. I passed the French captain, Serge Blanco, somewhere in the Sydney Football Stadium scarcely half-an-hour before the first Test began. He stopped, said hello, and we had a friendly chat for a few minutes. It was good to see him again, for Serge is one of those guys who demonstrates time and again the friendship aspect of rugby. This was a startling contrast to what happened when I went into the Australian dressing-room some time before the start of that match to greet Paul Carozza, the guy who had taken my place in the Wallaby side. As soon as I walked in, it quickly became apparent to me that I wasn't wanted in that room by some people. I might have played countless matches with some of them, but that didn't mean a thing; I wasn't in the chosen side that day and they didn't want me in there with them. Strange, really, and perhaps it reinforced my view that some people take the game far too seriously.

That day, for the first time in a long while, I felt alien to the whole Australian rugby set-up. As I thought about how a genuine attempt to wish a guy well had been all but thrown back in my face, I felt increasingly isolated. It seemed that my style of rugby and my attitude to the game was dying. During that match, Michael Lynagh must have kicked away 95 per cent of the possession the Wallabies won. And, perhaps for the first time in my entire life, I felt glad I was not wearing a Wallaby shirt that day.

If you love your country and you love the idea of playing for the Wallabies anything like as much as I do, then you would understand that even to think such a thing, let alone voice it, hurts me deeply. But all I could have done that day was to hang around out on the wing and get cold. Or I could have been caught up in the middle of a brawl started by Peter FitzSimons, which was a disgrace to the good name of rugby. It was quite obvious that Peter had played countless matches against some of the French players while playing for Brive and had a grudge to settle. He wanted to prove that he was an important player, big on the Australian rugby scene. But for those watching this shocking fight, like myself, it was not a pretty sight. I'm sure 39,000 people watching it with me would agree.

Bearing all that in mind, it is no wonder I feel that friendship is the greatest thing about the game. When you think about matches like that first Test, which are pretty awful both to watch and to play in, then you know there must be something else. And believe me, at that time I was badly in need of the knowledge that there were other qualities associated with the game, because I was far from in love with the idea that playing Test rugby was the ultimate goal. I didn't feel like representing the Wallabies because of the way they were playing. That is an awful thing to have to admit, but it was true. For some reason, I had just lost interest. Everything seemed to have changed; a lot of the guys I played alongside when I started were no longer there; instead there were a lot of young guys, different faces, different personalities. I didn't really know them and they were different characters to get along with. Maybe it was all to do with my general feelings, but I was on a real low around that time.

To meet guys like Jacques Fouroux, warm and friendly as ever, and Serge Blanco I found refreshing. It was hard to find a couple of Aussies who showed that kind of spirit and friendship. It was funny that after the game, as I waited outside the Sydney Football Stadium, I was approached by more French players – Lafond, Mesnel, Blanco again, Fouroux and five or six other players – and felt more a part of the French side because of the way they treated me. I spoke to only one Australian player. Yet the French had lost that day!

Sensing that kind of alienation from your own country isn't the most pleasant of experiences, but maybe I'm always going to be the loner, in rugby and in life. I had a long chat with the England captain Will Carling after we played for the Barbarians at Leicester, just after Christmas 1989. Will told me that England would never have chosen me, had I been born English, because I took too many chances. He said their philosophy was that if you get the ball in your own 22, nine times out of ten you kick it out. And usually ten out of ten. But I've always believed the best place from which to launch an attack is your own 22, precisely because the opposition are not expecting it. That's half the battle.

I have provided a few illustrations in this chapter of officialdom's less impressive side, and I want to close with a few supplementary remarks on that theme. It is my opinion that things have got to change in rugby; the authorities must start looking after the players. There should be two or three senior players from a current international team on a general committee of that union, offering their thoughts from the playing point of view. And why should the players not receive a minimum of six tickets for each international they play in, more pairs of boots and more leisure wear? It is a degrading spectacle to see players scrambling around trying to pick up a last couple of tickets a day or two before an international for the remaining members of their family or close friends who want to be there. At present a player is given only two tickets for Test matches, which means that if you have a family of six, you have to buy the rest. There always seems to be a quibble when the players want something. A lot of the guys see a Test match as their chance to pay back bosses who have been generous at work about time off. So maybe they want to ask five guys from the office with their wives, or even six, which means twelve extra tickets.

There was a Test match in Australia not too long ago when the players asked the ARU for 200 tickets. They were told they would have to buy them and were willing to do so, but when it came to it, their allowance was trimmed to 100, about six each. Yet I have never come across a committee man anywhere in the rugby-playing world moaning about an inadequate supply of tickets for the big matches. Strange, that. On the question of gear, look at the situation in France. The 1990 French tourists to Australia arrived resplendent in a tour uniform specially provided by Lacoste, the leading French clothing manufacturers. They had the lot: jackets, ties, shirts, sweaters, cardigans . . . you name it, it was there. I wish the ARU would line up a deal like that for the Wallabies when we go on tour.

The lack of ideas coming from many of these committees of national unions disturbs me. They seem to have little notion of how to promote the game in a great many cases, and there is always a wall between committee men and players. It is a suspicion, a total reluctance to involve players in the decision-making process. I am not saying I am the best player in Australian rugby, or that I merit special treatment, but I am the most senior and therefore perhaps entitled to some communication of views, both my own and those of the team as a whole. But this idea finds little favour in official circles. I am therefore drawn irresistibly to the view that Rugby Union in Australia will continue to lose many of its best players to the professional code simply because it does not know how to treat its players like human beings.

During the era of the mid to late 1980s, we had a spell when very few good Union players went to Rugby League. But then the floodgates opened and we lost another big group: Matthew and Brad Burke, Brett Papworth, Andrew Leeds, Ricky Stuart, James Grant, Michael Cook, Scott Gourlay, Matt Parish, Steve Lidbury and a few others. This constant drain means Australia will never have its best team available to put on to the paddock for a Rugby Union international. Was it a coincidence that between 1984 and 1987 we lost hardly anyone of note? No way. The reason was that we had a national coach at that time who was determined that his players would be looked after. Alan Jones made sure his players stayed by helping them and considering their views. He had the contacts and knew people to whom he could turn for jobs. In that respect, Alan Jones was excellent.

Of course, the main reason why New Zealand's best players have not turned to League for so many years is that they are being looked after. John Gallagher was made an offer he couldn't refuse and besides, it gave him the chance to go back to his own country where his parents still live. But for years, certain people in New Zealand made sure that the best players remained in Rugby Union and were therefore available for the All Blacks.

It is worth equating the situation in Australia with that of France. There, the leading clubs such as Racing Club, Toulouse, Agen, Béziers, Narbonne and Toulon are backed by the local councils or towns. Béziers now play, I understand, in a magnificent new stadium built and funded by the local municipality. The flow of funds does not stop there, either. Overseas guys who have played club rugby in France have reported how much they received for their services, and when the money was paid. I understand that they have been given 25 per cent on signature of their contract, 50 per cent halfway through the season and the remaining 25 per cent at the end of the season. It forms a basic salary, as much as $25,000 (£10,000) in some instances. And in the case of the best French internationals, you could double that sum and be somewhere near the amount they receive. This has been known for some years, it is nothing new. There is money in Italian rugby, as I have already explained. Yet the ARU baulks at the idea that a guy who has won 50 caps should pick up a measly 1500 bucks for a promotion. We live in another world.

Everything, or at least far too much, is second-class for the players. And although revolutions happen in other walks of life, it is hard to see many occurring in rugby. The authorities have this classic cop-out line as regards the players: 'If you don't like it, go to League' is their great excuse. What kind of logical, coherent thinking is involved in that sort of retort? Does it further the aims and ambitions, the quality of the amateur code? No way. The trouble is that all the players in Rugby Union are regarded as dispensable. Even if you retire early, like Mark Ella did, they don't say, 'What's wrong, can we help in some way?'. They just give you a pat on the back to help you on your way! When Mark played his last game for Randwick, against the English club, Bath, he had played for Randwick for ten years, captained Australia, was club captain and a great ambassador for the game. In the after-dinner speeches, the Randwick president stood up and said a few words about Mark and presented him with a wet-weather jacket, which he said was for his achievements over the previous ten years. I doubt whether it would have cost much more than $20 or $30 (£8 or £12). As Mark returned to his seat, he said jokingly: 'I've always wanted one of these!'.

I thought it was absolutely disgusting that a player of the calibre of Mark Ella, who had given so much to the game and especially to the spectators at Randwick, should be given as poor a gift as that. Am I alone in thinking that something of real and lasting value such as an inscribed gold watch would have been more suitable?

When someone retires, no attempt is made to find out if there is some major reason for his decision. That is one of the strengths and weaknesses of rugby: a strength, because the game allows freedom of expression; weakness, because the authorities can just turn to someone else. There is always the awareness in the back of their minds that another player will come along. They don't care how much time or devotion you have given to the game or what you might have done for rugby. The attitude is, 'If you don't want to play, no worries, mate; we'll find someone who does'.

In places like Britain, you could put 15 cardboard cut-outs dressed in England shirts on to the field at Twickenham and you would still get the place sold out, as long as there were 15 opposite them dressed in the red shirts of Wales. That's the position from which the authorities know they can dictate the terms. It's healthy yet it's desperately unhealthy, too.

I think that trust funds should be set in place for the Rugby Union player of the future. It would be too late to affect me, so I am not saying this for personal profit. I see nothing wrong in a situation some time in the future in which five per cent of the gate at every Test match were put aside for a trust fund for the players when they finally retire. Those who stay in

Union the longest should receive the most. That would encourage guys to remain in the game rather than clearing off to Rugby League when a few thousand bucks are waved under their noses. It would strengthen the Union game and do no kind of damage whatsoever to its amateur ethics. Yet it is frowned upon by those in authority.

I am not a braggart, but nor am I a fool. I am aware, to some extent, of my market value and of the fact that my name has brought some people to matches in my time. Other players are the same. Is it really presumptive to state that a great many people have paid good money to go and see a guy like Mark Ella, or Serge Blanco, or John Kirwan play a game of rugby? After all, I would. But all the authorities give you in recognition of this are stingy expenses and a pat on the back which says, 'See you next time; and then you can make some more money for us'! Alan Jones was right . . . players as mobile banks, he called us. It was never better put.

CHAPTER
—9—

ALAN JONES AND ME

When Alan Jones was appointed coach of the Australian national side, I was filled with deep foreboding, fear even. Four years later, in the days before Jones' sacking from the position, I did something I shall regret for the rest of my life. In between, Alan Jones paid me the highest compliment possible: he called me the Bradman of rugby. And yet there were times when I could happily have wrung his neck for him!

To this day, I have never come across a man with so many varied talents, a man who invoked so many differing emotions among those with whom he came into contact. Jones is a brilliant orator, a magnificent motivator; a man with a brain which left me and most other sportsmen for dead when it was charged up and really racing. He might not have been the world's most knowledgeable guy on rugby, but he taught the Wallabies a priceless quality – how to win. And no coach could ever do more for his side than Alan Jones did for Australia. He never stopped working to secure the next victory; he became almost obsessive about success. Ultimately, that obsession probably led to his downfall, because one of Jones' faults was his inability to accept defeat and failure. Because he worked on so high an octane, he could not understand the failure of others to operate constantly at those lofty levels.

It is my intention in these pages to provide a balanced view on my times with Alan Jones. For those who just want to see his blood spilled, what follows may be a disappointment. I feel free to make honest criticism of him as he criticised me at times during our association, but equally I want to make it very clear that I have a deep respect for what the man achieved during his tenure. I shall also say something I have never before admitted to anyone about his final days as Wallaby coach, but that is to get ahead of my story.

Jones won the nomination for Wallaby coach early in 1984. There had been dissatisfaction following the series in France which we lost 1-0, the other Test having been drawn. It was a pretty miserable tour, and at the end of it a lot of people back home seemed to think that Bob Dwyer should pay the ultimate price for defeat, a view which I found hard to understand. I knew Bob Dwyer very well by this time and felt that he had begun to mould the team together. He was the one I had started with, so it was perfectly natural for there to be some empathy between him and myself. But that was as far as it could go, because I was only a player, and a young one at that. When the result of the vote was announced and Jones had beaten Dwyer, I was upset. However, I knew it was my duty to get on with whoever was going to be coach, to play the game and do my absolute best if I were chosen. If you play for Australia, you are all in it together. There is no way you should ever discriminate against a certain guy because he comes from another club or he was given the job at the expense of someone you got on with. That would be crazy, for we all have the same goal in life: to enjoy success with the Wallabies.

The first Test Australia played under Jones was against Fiji in Suva. I found it rather strange, because one of the reasons advanced for Dwyer's sacking was the fact that he tended to pick his Randwick players. Then Jones, who had been Manly coach and a successful one at that – he took them to the Sydney premiership title in 1983 – came in and started choosing Manly players such as Williams, Reynolds, Black, FitzSimons and Calcraft. But I figured that any coach would probably go back to those he knew best. It isn't a criticism of Jones, but equally I feel it should not have counted against Dwyer.

So we flew to Suva, won there, and then came back to prepare for the tour by New Zealand in which they would play three Tests. I have recounted elsewhere how this series developed, but the relevance here is the way Jones set about preparing us. He wanted to beat New Zealand every bit as much as we did, and we set out with that task uppermost in our minds. He concentrated on basic skills, ensuring that they were right and filling us with confidence. We quickly realised that this guy was something else when it came to motivation. He would tell us constantly that we could do it and I enjoyed that. There is nothing like the experience of going out on to the field for a Test match feeling deep down that you are a better team than your opponents and that if you concentrate, work hard and don't do anything seriously wrong, you will win. Jones hallmarked that quality; no Wallaby side under him ever went into a match under-prepared or lacking motivation for the fray.

Training was very hard, tough even, but that suited me fine, too. He told us we were there to play for Australia, not to bum around, and that sounded fair enough to me. We trained very, very hard and reaped the benefits. I don't think I have ever trained as hard before or since under any other man in rugby football. It was very physical training, too. When things did not go well, Jones would quickly become pretty aggressive. He was very critical, but then I think he knew what we could do and felt entitled to pick us up if we dipped below the standards he set. And those standards were certainly high. He was determined to get the best out of the players, and sometimes the best way to do that is to pick on them and say, 'I know what you can do and you haven't done it yet. Do it properly'.

At first with a new coach, you listen to whatever he does or says and try and abide by it. It's the circus trainer teaching the lion new tricks; the beast is probably a bit intrigued to start with and goes along with it. I went to training and listened carefully to what Jones had to say. And why not – this was only my third year of international rugby and I was still young and learning. It was true that the side as a whole was more experienced – players like Mark Ella, Slacky, Roger Gould, Griggie, Steve Williams and Chris Roche were still around and had been there for quite a while. By contrast, I was still very much a novice.

We quickly realised that Jones would have a very different approach off the field to Bob Dwyer. Bob would mix socially, have a drink or two with the boys after a game and join in the laughs. It was totally different with Alan. He never drank with us, and after most matches he would never be around. His relationship with the team was more like that between a schoolmaster and his pupils whereas Bob Dwyer was really like a fellow player.

I don't see myself as the judge of these two, quite different methods. If it were me, I think I would tend to follow more of Bob's approach because I would want to form a close relationship with my players and make sure they understood me and the way I worked. But if you look at the form book and see the results Jonesy achieved working it his way, you cannot criticise him. And it is an incontrovertible necessity for a coach to have respect from his players. I don't think he can be a friend first and a coach second. He must be, above all else, a coach and then, if he wishes to be, a friend. I'm not saying that a coach should be out drinking with his players all the time, but now and then it probably does not hurt. The next morning he can still get at you if you don't train well – that is the unwritten law of the relationship. A coach will do what he sees fit.

When Jones took over I was apprehensive: you never know whether you will be picked or not when there is a 'new broom'. I was young and I had a lot of faults, one of which was that my tackling was pretty ordinary.

But Jones started from scratch with the whole team. We did a lot of physical work and a lot of tackling (I left all my tackling on the training paddock!). Through that, there is no doubt that we gained a great deal more confidence and understanding. We were secure in the knowledge that we were building on solid basics and that was invaluable.

Jones always worked extremely hard for Australia. And it has always been obvious that if he does something he does it extremely well. The results did not come about by chance or accident; the amount of work he put in ensured there would be an end product. He worked us so hard that at times the last thing you felt like facing was another Alan Jones training session. But we won, and it doesn't matter how much effort or sweat it has taken to get there if you end up winning. Even at international level, you have to put in the graft to achieve success. Simply having the talent and thinking that just turning up will be enough is wide of the mark. Jones led the way when it came to input.

If you are the boss of a company, you have to be there all the time, demonstrating your commitment. You cannot take afternoons off to go out on the golf course because if you do, the staff immediately think they can do the same. In our business, you cannot train twice a week and expect to be the best in the world. You have to drive yourself constantly to reach a peak which sets you apart from the rest. Jones always did that with us, and he emphasised the need for that supreme level of fitness and condition.

Alan was a perfectionist. He knew what he wanted and he knew what he could probably get out of us. He set himself the highest standards and expected us to match them. If we didn't, then we were told in no uncertain terms that we had fallen short of expectation. For example, if you made a mistake or something was not right, you would talk about it and sort it out. That might mean a conversation somewhere at 11.30 at night, or another 20 minutes on the traning ground when you were supposed to be heading for a reception with the local Mayor and were already half-an-hour late. Jones didn't mind about that; he saw his job as getting all the errors ironed out. Nothing would be left to chance.

You might think that goal-kicking is something the expert can concentrate on himself, even that it is an art that cannot be coached in the normal sense of the word. But Alan Jones never subscribed to that theory. He would stand behind the goalposts or alongside the kicker and study his action. If you were snatching at the kick he could tell you, and if you lacked rhythm in your kicks, he saw that, too. Each kicker in the team might take more than 30 pots at goal once formal training had ended, but Jones never shirked his commitment. If it was pouring with rain and he had to stand out in it just watching a guy boot a ball over the crossbar, then he would do it and not even think about the discomfort. He told us countless times that he knew a great many guys in the Wallaby squad could get a lot out of rugby, so he would encourage them all he could to ensure that their potential was realised.

He helped me a considerable amount with my confidence. The rugby supporter might find it strange that a guy who has played over 50 times for his country ever lacked confidence but I did, especially in my early years. In 1986, just before we played France in Sydney, Jones took me aside and said, 'The public out there don't think you can play full-back. Some don't even think you can play rugby. Go out and prove the lot of them wrong, prove you can tackle because I know you can'. Some people might think that added more pressure to my game because I went on to the field wanting to tackle anything that moved. But it never harmed me, and it showed how Jones could help boost your confidence. However, he was often the one who said in the newspapers that my tackling was suspect. It seemed that he was applying a reverse psychology.

Some of the talks the man gave were unbelievable, they were so good (sometimes I didn't even understand what he was talking about!). Inspirational was the word. His planning and preparation for matches were outstanding, always. He must have done meticulous research. He would get you at the ground before a game and pick the opposition apart. 'OK Campo,' he would say, 'your man is no good going to the left, so go for that side and you will be right.' Preparation was honed down to a fine art because there was not a weakness in an opposing player he would not know about. It was like fighting a war when you had broken the enemy's secret code and knew exactly where the point of his next attack was going to be. The value of that in terms of confidence is impossible to exaggerate.

He drilled into us the need to believe in ourselves. He was solely concerned with trying to instil confidence into us and he succeeded handsomely. Everyone came to believe totally in themselves and their ability to go out and play well. Behind us all the time was this voice saying, 'You can do it, believe it, you are easily good enough. Believe in yourselves'. I always knew whether I had played well or badly. If it had been a good performance Jonesy would pat me on the back, but if it was a bad one he wouldn't come near me! Under Alan Jones, I can honestly say I never once went on to the field for a Test match fearing the opposition. Never. Sometimes, though, we used to fear what he would say when we got back to the dressing-room! He certainly didn't shy away from showing his aggression when things had not gone well for us. I think he found it extremely hard to accept anything less than victory.

If we lost, he would say we had let him down as though it was a personal affront to his dignity. When he called me 'the Bradman of rugby football' it was an extraordinary compliment to pay anyone, and it left me quite stunned when I first heard him use it. Higher praise would not be possible for a rugby player in Australia, and it really made me think. But the trouble was that when I made a mistake, and especially if it had been expensive, he would throw this phrase back at me, saying, 'I told people you were the Bradman of rugby and now you have let me down'. But that was ridiculous. For a start, I hadn't made the mistake deliberately, and what Alan seemed loath to accept was that I was like everyone else, just another human being capable of erring. After all, even Bradman was out for a duck occasionally. But Alan couldn't seem to handle this fact, and in time he came to expect perhaps too much of his players. This was especially true at the 1987 World Cup. It seemed impossible for Alan to grasp the reality that where human beings are involved, you can train and train and train them until you are nearly dead with exhaustion, but still you will never eliminate their capacity for making mistakes. You can eradicate an enormous number of errors through hard work and preparation, and the Wallabies proved that during Jones' time as coach, but of course we were never totally free of them, and that was something with which Jonesy seemed unable to come to terms.

Many people continue to wonder, to this day, whether that Wallaby side of 1984 would have been as successful without him. That is always going to be an imponderable, but the facts are that he was there, he was firmly at the helm and we won. We will never know whether it might have been different under someone else.

Alan had so many good, positive attributes. For example, I cannot imagine that any coach has ever looked after his players better than he did. He would take guys out to dinner and not dream of doing anything but paying for it all himself. And you did not get only the set menu, either; you had just what you wanted. If anyone had any kind of problem, he knew that Alan would willingly sort it out. He was always there, always available, always ready and willing to help. Yet the other side of the guy was that he often blew hot and cold. He made what I thought was a mistake by treating us like schoolchildren sometimes. He had been brought up to believe in the headmaster role and he brought that approach with him when he became Wallaby coach.

In the early days, when I could see how motivational this guy was, I suppose you could say I was as much of a Jones boy as anyone else. In my mind, anyway, whatever he said, I did. But after a few years many of the guys started to turn away from his ideas, and all he was left with were the few who have remained Jones fans to this day. There is nothing wrong with that, but for many of us the time came when we began to feel weary of the Jones creed.

It is my firm belief that all coaches, whoever they are, have a natural lifespan in terms of a certain job. I have never believed that a coach, however successful, can go on for year after year, doing the same job and putting across basically the same message. Someone somewhere will probably cite some sport which proves me wrong, but in my experience, it is human nature for a player to stop listening after a while. It's a bit like the demonstration of the safety devices on aircraft, explained so carefully by the stewardess before you take off. The first dozen times you fly, perhaps more, you hang on every word spoken. And while it is beyond dispute that you *should* continue to listen just as carefully thereafter, the fact is you don't. This can be seen whenever you take a flight with a large number of regular business travellers. They sit there, reading their newspapers or working on papers while the stewardess goes through her bit about the oxygen supply and how to undo the safety belt, and it is clear that because they have heard it a hundred times before their level of concentration has diminished considerably.

This is how it tended to be for me with Jonesy, and I would say that his influence on the Wallabies as a whole also diminished in this respect. His stirring words started to lose their effect after a while. That, and the fact that he worked himself up to such a fever pitch of preparation and intensity that he found it increasingly difficult to accept the failings of mere mortals, made some of us start to switch off. I hate to say it, but perhaps it had all become just too intense, too serious. He had got us up there and it was as though he then expected us never to lose. We had done all the preparatory work and perhaps we thought we were good enough never to be beaten. But neither sport nor life is like that.

It is my belief that Jones thought we could not fail. I suspect, too, that he felt he had made us, and if we let him down, he feared the public would blame him and say he was a bad coach. There is no doubt that the side was increasingly regarded as *his* team. He was forever being interviewed by every form of the media, talking about matches and players. You could see him on television talking about the team or a big match coming up, you could hear him on radio and read his further thoughts in all the newspapers. He had an extremely high profile which extended to rugby as a whole, and that is something very, very few people have managed in Australia in recent years. Of course, people were right to think it was his team and it worked well because he put so much effort into it. But this intensity created even more expectation, demanded ever finer victories and outstanding successes. There could be no room for failure. And eventually, that was the downfall of Jones.

Against this extremely well-educated, learned man who could come up with words some of us had simply never heard of, a guy like myself could not even begin to compete. I had very little education at all in the sense of achieving major academic standards. I had no riches of a financial or intellectual nature. Putting it bluntly, I wasn't in the same street as Jonesy in any sense, and I quickly figured that out. So I would listen, hoping to learn and develop. It seemed not only a sensible policy but the only policy. I was even in a different class to team-mates like Roger Gould and Michael Hawker – I was a nobody, I hardly knew what was happening in the world. When someone like me has as dominant a coach as Jones, he keeps quiet and listens.

Given these circumstances, most of what I was told I believed. But after a while, even I began to say to myself, 'Hold it, I'm not that stupid. I'm not swallowing everything this guy tells me'. There was a danger that Jones was having too great a say in our lives. One of Alan's greatest attributes, as I have said, was that he was always there to help you. All you had to do was make a telephone call and he'd say, 'Leave it to me, I'll sort it out'. This took my understanding of the relationship between a coach and his players into a new stratosphere. But after returning from New Zealand in 1986, I found that this relationship could become overbearing. I was still down in Queanbeyan, and needed to find a job. I told Alan about my problem and he promised to get back to me. But time went by and I heard nothing. Weeks passed, perhaps six or even eight, and I still hadn't anything fixed up. At almost exactly the same time Bob Dwyer, who was then coach of Randwick, rang me up about something and I happened to mention to him that I was looking for a job. Bob immediately said, 'Come up to Sydney, I'll get you fixed up'. I flew up, went for an interview and got the job. I think I even started the next week.

The day after I accepted the job, Alan Jones rang up. I told him what had happened and he said 'You were not supposed to speak to anyone until you had spoken to me'. I pointed out that six or eight weeks had gone by since we'd had the conversation about work – this wasn't altogether surprising, mind you, because Alan tended to cram more into his life than most people would manage in three or four lives. As I hadn't worked for six weeks I was getting desperate. Alan didn't like the fact that I had accepted an offer and told me so. But I couldn't understand why I was being criticised for making a decision which, after all, affected my future. You cannot expect so much just because you are a rugby coach. When we started to train for the World Cup in January 1987 I could sense that Jonesy was not very happy with either my training or the fact that I was by then living and working in Sydney and playing for Randwick.

A rift appeared in our relationship because I had made a decision on my own without his influence. It was perhaps an indication of the influence Alan wanted over my life and I reckon I wasn't the only one to notice it. I deal with the 1987 World Cup, and the build-up to the 1991 tournament, elsewhere in this book, but I'd like to include here some thoughts on the

1987 competition as it related to Jonesy. Of course, the pressures were high on Jonesy and on all the Wallabies at that time. He was the one up there, talking to the journalists and raising expectations. We had whacked the Brits and the Irish three years earlier, demolished the French in Sydney in 1986 (actually, they outscored us by three tries to one yet somehow lost 27-14!) and won a Test series against New Zealand, in the Shaky Isles, the previous year. Expectations were high that Australia would do well in, and perhaps even win, the first-ever World Cup. A lot was at stake, for Jonesy and for all of us. And not only did the pressures quickly become apparent – so, too, did the mistakes.

The first error was that Alan decided we should train in the afternoons (normally we were used to training in the mornings), chiefly because he was busy each morning working on his radio show in Sydney. That might have made sense to him as he arranged his hectic schedule, but for us, forced to hang around half the day before we could do anything in terms of real work, it was dreadful. For five weeks, we hung around the hotel, kicking our heels and not knowing what to do with ourselves for hours and hours. You don't want to stay in bed all morning; your natural inclination is to get up. But to do what? If we had trained early, some of us would have done extra training afterwards, probably weights in the gym, but as it was, we didn't want to tire ourselves out before proper training began. I suppose there was always Jonesy's radio show to listen to! Admittedly, some mornings Alec Evans would run a training session, but it would be mainly to get us out of our hotel rooms. And we always trained in the afternoons, even on those days, so we couldn't do too much in the morning sessions.

Of course, by the time we began training, Jones had been hard at work for hours and was probably already physically weary. If he'd had a bad morning, he was liable to take it out on us at training. I felt, and I was not alone by any means, that in a situation where you were dealing with an amateur rugby team as opposed to a group of blokes picking up thousands of dollars for being there, this was unacceptable. I say to this day that it was a mistake.

Another error Jonesy made, in my opinion anyway, was to hang on for too long to certain players. He was too loyal and ultimately paid the price. I'm not going to slag off players here by naming the ones who stayed too long, nor would I say that they cost us the World Cup because it simply isn't true. Every player involved, myself included, must accept part of the blame for Australia's eventual failure to win the trophy. But I think the general view was that we had seen the best of some players, and I don't disagree with that verdict. Most of the team had been together for three or four years and the World Cup probably came 12 months too late for us. Had it been staged in 1986, around the time we were doing the most difficult thing in the rugby-playing world – beating the All Blacks in New Zealand – I don't doubt that we would have won it.

Perhaps another factor in our failure was that we had trained ourselves into the ground. We had been hard at it on the training field since January that year, and the World Cup did not begin until 17 May, with a month of intense competition to follow. We had started when everyone in Australia was on the beach in January, and there were training sessions on public holidays at weekend camps. We trained and we trained: we flogged ourselves before matches. There was no rest, not even when it seemed clear that some of the guys needed to have a break because they were sore from running all the time. Maybe it all meant just that bit too much to our coach.

You pay a price for being different in life, never mind just in rugby. I get a lot of criticism because I try to do the unpredictable thing, the entertaining thing. For me, enjoyment comes first, winning is next in importance and then entertaining. I think crowds know I can play, even when I spend 80 minutes on a rugby field without showing what I can really do because the opportunity does not present itself. I like to show my versatility, but even I accept that that cannot always be achieved. However, I have to say that towards the end of Alan Jones' period as Wallaby coach I was not enjoying my rugby. There was too much pressure on us and I was being abused.

Alan began to stifle people with all the pressure. He made a very bad blue after we lost the semi-final of the 1987 World Cup when he said in front of a player and his girlfriend: 'I made a big mistake today, maybe the biggest mistake of my career. I should not have picked so and so. I knew I should not have picked him'. I know who that player was but I'm not going to name him. He knows, too, because he heard the story himself – not from me, I hasten to add. The point is, that should not have been said, especially in front of a player and his girlfriend. Where is the trust, the loyalty between the coach and his players that Jonesy had drummed into us for so much of his career, in such a remark? Jones had started his coaching career with the Wallabies by telling us that he would never single out anyone or blame an individual for losing.

Yet he had been doing just that for some time. In 1986, during our Test series in New Zealand, we hit rock bottom when we lost the second Test at Dunedin by a single point, 13-12. We had won the first Test by an identical margin; this time, however, the single-point defeat meant we had not wrapped up the series as we had promised ourselves we would do. I'll be quite honest: I made mistakes in both matches. At Wellington, where the first Test was held, I threw a poor pass towards Matt Burke. Joe Stanley gathered it after the ball bounced and the All Blacks eventually scored. We still won, but only just. Then Dunedin gave us a traditional welcome: lousy cold and rain tumbling out of leaden skies. Very reminiscent of Sydney or

Brisbane – I don't think! I was playing full-back and dropped a few bombs the All Blacks put up to me. I had a far from spectacular game and we ended up losing.

Afterwards, I went in to have a shower and I could see that Jonesy was very upset. We all were. Slacky, our captain, looked as though he'd lost a close relative. But what right did our coach have to tell the other players while I was in the shower: 'Don't worry, fellows, you played without a full-back today'. I found that out two days later and you can imagine how I felt. Anyway, when we got back to the hotel, I went in to see Jones. I knew I'd played badly and I wanted to tell him I was sorry. I mumbled something about it not being my day, but he just went over the top. He said, 'I told the papers you were the Bradman of rugby – now you've let me down. Tomorrow we were going to go skiing, now that's off and we've got a hell of a job in front of us. The series should have been won by now'. He said he felt like packing his bags and going home. He said people back home would think we were the Greg Normans of rugby – although Norman had been unlucky on a few occasions, it had seemed as though he could never win.

He said a lot more, too, until Nick Farr-Jones walked past the room, caught a snatch of the conversation and came in to save me. The diatribe had gone on for five or ten minutes and I found it pretty degrading. It was as if I'd deliberately played poorly and lost the match for the guys. No one goes out there to lose, especially if they're an Australian in New Zealand, but things sometimes go wrong (how come it always happens to me?). I felt then that Alan was becoming far too intense – maybe because it was his name and his job on the line, not ours. He was the high-profile guy, so when something went wrong, he was the one they blamed. But this was surely his fault: it was rarely the Wallabies and Alan Jones, but Alan Jones and the Wallabies; and quite often, it was Alan Jones and his team, which was pretty sickening.

I left that room feeling hurt and humiliated. I did something I virtually never do, as I said much earlier: I went out and got drunk. Outside in the Dunedin night the rain was trickling down the windows and the wind was blowing. It was cold and horrible, which exactly reflected my mood. The drops of rain on the windows could have been tears in my soul. I felt fed up and wanted to go home. It could have been an interesting flight had I found myself sitting next to Jonesy all the way back to Australia! Did I deserve that tongue-lashing? To this day, I don't think so. Maybe it would have been the ideal therapy for some guys, but Jonesy had summed me up very badly if he thought it would inspire me. It depressed me utterly.

I don't mind admitting that I am a sensitive guy: I might show a bit of bravado at times but it's not the real me emerging at moments like that. I hate being upset by people in those circumstances, especially if it is not justified. And are a few errors made on a sports field by an amateur reason enough to launch that kind of verbal assault on someone? No way. I felt as though I couldn't care less whether I played another match for the Wallabies, or indeed any other game of rugby. Here I was, putting in all this time, commitment and effort, and my reward was a mouthing-off. I didn't deserve it and no one else would have done, in my view.

Of course, I knew that it had only happened because Alan had become so intense in his desire to see us win. He seemed to want victory more than us and had adopted almost a fanatical desire to beat the All Blacks. Perhaps he remembered 1984 when we had let them off the hook so badly, or perhaps he just felt, like most Australians, that it's important to beat the All Blacks before almost anyone. That was true of the players, but maybe we could look at it in a slightly more detached light and realise that, at the end of the day, it was only a rugby match. I felt increasingly as Jones' reign as coach continued, that he was unable to recognise the difference between the importance of victory and the realisation that it was, in the end, just a game. Maybe that was a direct result of the amount of work and effort, the time and commitment he put into it. No one could have done more on our behalf to make victory possible but when it didn't happen, Alan seemed unable to accept it. I simply could not see how mouthing-off one or any number of players was going to bring victory nearer. It seemed utterly counter-productive.

No way had it been my intention to make mistakes in that important game, any more than Greg Norman would have set out to play the round he produced on the third day of the British Open golf tournament at St Andrews in 1990. He was level with the overnight leader Nick Faldo after two of the four rounds, and everyone expected Norman and Faldo to go right to the wire over the last two rounds. Instead, Greg shot a dreadful round of 76 and disappeared out of sight as a likely contender for the title. Imagine Greg's dismay at what happened that day, when he, like me, had had so many hopes for a good outcome. But would he have deserved a tongue-lashing from someone when he got back to his hotel just because his form had deserted him? Of course not.

There were sequels to that incident. The first came the next morning, when I awoke feeling like death warmed up. When you are not used to alcohol its effect is multiplied if you do climb into it. I was as crook as a dog all the next day. I didn't feel a lot better, either, when I heard the team chosen for the next match, against Southland at Invercargill. Michael Lynagh was picked at full-back instead of me and given the captaincy, while I was put on the wing. Lynagh then spent the training sessions telling me what to do and where to stand. That really pissed me off. Then I pulled a sciatic nerve in my leg. That compounded the pain and humiliation; I couldn't handle it all, it had become too much. I was so sick of everything. I guess you could say that the love affair with Jonesy had well and truly ended by then – in my view, he had gone too far. Sometimes, winning and the pursuit of it takes away the pleasure of rugby and just playing the game.

Then the story got out that I'd been savaged verbally by our coach over my poor form at Dunedin. Jonesy denied it and, when we got back to Sydney, rang me up and said he wanted me to go on his radio show to confirm it hadn't happened. What the hell do you do in circumstances like that – tell your national coach to get lost? So, tamely and regrettably, I went along with the charade because I had no choice. I would probably never have played for Australia again if I'd taken the guy to task in public. I was trapped. But it deepened the hurt and humiliation of the whole thing and I maintain to this day that Jonesy was wrong to treat me that way.

But to finish the story, of course I stayed for the rest of the tour and played on the winning side in the third Test in Auckland. We clinched the series 2-1, only the fourth team ever to win a Test series in New Zealand, a fair achievement. And when you win, it is as though the previous mistakes never happened in some people's estimation. It's amazing, isn't it – you lose one Test and you are accused of being the worst player ever known, and you're told it was all your fault. Then you win the next Test and people expect you to forget everything that was said. A lot of people would, too, but I couldn't. I didn't forget it then, and I haven't to this day. This wasn't the first time such a thing had happened. When we went to Cardiff to play the Sport Aid Sevens we were winning easily near the end of one game against inferior opposition. We had another match coming up 15 minutes later, so when I got the ball, I ran down the field at half-pace. We won the match, but Jones gave me a dressing-down after the game for my lack of speed.

Well, we went at full pace to flog Ireland and were told we had done well. But then we lost against England. Glen Ella threw a pass which went over my head and they picked it up to score. Jones went through me afterwards. He said some of my decisions had been bad and asked what I had been thinking about. One of my colleagues, Ross Reynolds, came into the shower when I was there and said, 'Mate, how do you cop all this shit? I've never heard anyone cop so much in my life'.

I hate losing, I really do – especially in big matches like that World Cup semi-final in 1987 after we had put in so much effort over so long a period of time. On the other hand, one team has to lose and it was a great game, one of the best anyone could recall. Surely that had to be some consolation? In that match Michael Lynagh broke the points-scoring record for a Wallaby and I broke the world record for the number of Test match tries with 25. But we would both have sacrificed those records for a victory. We couldn't, so that was it. We were always trying to live up to Alan's expectations of us as a team, but in the end they became so elevated that they were out of reach. Maybe they would have been for any side. We had all worked desperately hard as a unit to get where we were, and none had worked harder than Alan himself. But I think he forgot that with any team you can only go so far. There is no way you can always win everything. However good you become, there is always a team somewhere that is going to beat you sooner or later and deny you some glory.

In any top-class sport, you have to be realistic and accept the skills of your opponents. Sometimes, too, as a logical development of that argument, you have to accept you were beaten by a better side on the day. In that 1987 World Cup semi-final, France scored some great tries against us. They did ever so well. But Alan seemed too wrapped up in the misery of our defeat to recognise just how well the French had played. Perhaps all the months and years of dedication, work and endeavour on our behalf had brought about a weariness which could only be compounded by defeat, any defeat.

Yet, as I have said, there were plenty of good, indeed great, things about Alan. One of them was the way he could spot young talent and develop it on the world stage; he was formidable at that. In 1984, the Wallabies arrived in Britain assuming that Phillip Cox would be their number one scrum-half. The kid who had been included as number two, Nick Farr-Jones, seemed to be there only for the experience. But Jonesy clearly thought otherwise, and Nick not only played all the Tests on our Grand Slam tour but also made a significant contribution to our success. It was Jones at his best. There were plenty of others, too.

Steve Cutler was hardly playing first-grade rugby when apparently Jonesy rang him up soon after winning the nomination for coach and told him, 'You are going to be my number one line-out jumper on the tour of the UK in six months' time. Get yourself into shape and prepare for a great future', or words to that effect. And what a choice that was: 'Cuts' dominated the Brits and Irish in the line-outs and he too had a massive influence in our triumph. Matthew Burke, an unknown youngster when he arrived in Britain, also came through on that tour. And, later on, Jonesy picked a kid named Brett Papworth, who was potentially one of the greatest midfield backs Australian rugby has ever known, but who was sadly lost to the game when he turned professional. Again, Alan had spotted Pappie's genius and brought him through to the Wallaby side. His choice of Slacky as captain was also shrewd, and look how much he got out of Mark Ella. They were totally different characters, poles apart really, but you only have to see what a success Mark was on that tour to realise what an enormous amount Alan had to do with that.

On that 1984 tour, not only did we have a very good team, but we all knew what we were doing. We were pretty experienced as a side, but Jones gave us discipline; he taught us not to do anything stupid. Just play the game and win the matches, he would say. Without any hesitation, I would say that discipline was lacking before Jonesy came in, as I think it was also lacking in the Australian team of 1990.

I've said plenty about how Jonesy was out of order in some of the things he did during his time as Wallaby coach. Now it's time for me to put up my hands and admit that I was equally culpable in the part I played in his downfall as coach. I make no excuses for what I did because it was completely wrong.

When Alan lost the national coaching job, he made a serious allegation against me. He publicly accused me of telephoning certain influential people in Australian rugby circles and speaking against him. I am sad to admit that his allegation was perfectly correct. I was in Sydney at the time, I did do that and I now regret it deeply. I rang up a couple of people and said that I knew a number of players who would no longer play for the Wallabies if Alan Jones remained as coach. At the back of my mind was the thought that I could not face going through all that criticism again. And I probably would have retired from international rugby had Jonesy carried on as coach. I suspect some of the others would have felt the same way. But you get to a situation where you are scared of not being chosen, and I am sure Alan would not have continued to pick me had he remained as national coach. There would have been some reason why I was being left out, and I sensed that.

Although many players may not like a certain coach, they are not prepared to do anything about it, unless everyone joins them. I suppose you could say that I felt that it had come down to Alan Jones or me. If he stayed I went, and vice versa. It had become pretty black and white. What I did at the time I considered to be right, but with the benefit of hindsight, a quality which makes experts of us all too damned late, I know that action should never have been taken. I would never do it again. If a player rings someone up and says, 'Look, if he stays I am not playing any more', it is really nothing short of a form of blackmail.

I rang two or three people, and I admit that they could have been influential in deciding Alan's fate, a fact which makes me even less proud of my behaviour. But there were some players from Queensland who knew what I was doing, and I believe that in theory, at least, they were behind me. I didn't disclose their names: if anything had happened, I wanted to be sure that it would only be my fault, not to drag in someone else who had no. really wanted to be involved in the first place. All the same, I was being truthful when I said that there were other players who felt the same way as I did.

I don't think the eventual decision to remove Alan was taken because of what I said to anyone – I think he had done his time and there was a general wish for change – but I might have helped along his departure, if only by a fraction, a tiny percentage. And if that is the case, then I regret it.

I accept now that this was a knife in the back of Alan Jones; he may well have been on the blocks anyway, but that does not excuse my action. I'd like to say publicly to Alan that today, a few years on, and now that I am, I hope, a few years older and wiser, I am sorry for what I did. My apology is genuine.

I am happy to say that I have met Jonesy a few times since he finished as Wallaby coach. When we have bumped into each other in Sydney he has greeted me with courtesy and warmth. I'd like that situation to continue, despite what I have admitted in this chapter. I have confessed that I made a mistake in my action and I hope the apology will be accepted in the spirit in which it is offered. I still have a lot of respect for Alan Jones and what he did as Wallaby coach. Just look at the records and you'll see how successful he was as coach to Australia.

CHAPTER
— 10 —

THE WORLD CUP: 1987 AND 1991

It is possible to paint a unique picture of the rugby world at the 1991 World Cup in Britain, Ireland and France. High-profile players from all the main countries may be carrying bags sponsoring certain companies; they may be pictured in the match programmes advertising particular brands of clothing and they may be driving smart cars, sporting the name of the sponsoring garage down the side by the player's name. They may, too, have private contracts to represent major companies by speaking to clients, executives and generally promoting that company. And if they make a few thousand bucks at a tournament, which is sure to gross tens of millions of dollars, then the very best of luck to the lot of them. Yet these personal profits are as a pinprick seen in the context of the bags of dough the authorities will rake in from an event which has been described as the largest sports tournament staged in the British Isles since the 1966 soccer World Cup. And that is a long time ago.

The figures released well in advance of the tournament in terms of television sales, overseas rights, sponsoring companies' outlay and other assorted sources of cash were pretty impressive. Without a doubt, by kick-off at the first match on 3 October, a great deal more would have been amassed. Rugby was set to coin it at this event and I just hope that the people counting that money remember that it is the players who are the centre of attraction. No one is going to pay big sums for tickets to see the secretary of the Scottish Rugby Union or the President of the Irish Union taking their seats.

As for the event itself, it may be instructive to look back at 1987 and the lessons which were there to be learned at the first World Cup. That year proved to almost all the players that the idea of holding it in more than one country was as daft as a brush. Many of those in authority said so, too, after the tournament. Some players involved in the finals never even went to the country where the actual final was held. They played thousands of miles away in Australia, were beaten there and went home from there. They had no chance to taste any of the World Cup atmosphere in New Zealand.

This always seemed to me an absurd arrangement and it became steadily more incomprehensible as the tournament developed. Can you imagine, for example, the 1990 soccer World Cup, which was staged in Italy, holding half its matches in Sweden with the final in Rome? The comparison between Rome and Stockholm is appropriate, because the distance between the two cities is almost identical to that between Sydney, scene of one of the World Cup semi-finals in 1987 and Auckland, where the final was held. That is how crazy the whole idea actually was. As this was the first tournament, we swallowed our disapproval, recognising that any new event is bound to have its teething troubles and assuming that they will surely be sorted out next time. But in 1991 the World Cup was to be spread not over two countries as in 1987, but over five: England, Wales, Scotland, Ireland and France. I'm at a loss to understand the logic behind that.

I have no argument with the staging of the tournament in the British Isles and Ireland because there are four logical, deeply-established venues which make a perfectly compact, collective venue for the World Cup. But what on earth France has been dragged in for, I cannot imagine. While France competes with Britain and Ireland in the Five Nations Championship, it is otherwise treated as a perfectly separate country in that it makes and hosts overseas tours all of its own, without any link to the Four Home Unions. Australia toured there in 1989, New Zealand in 1990. There was no question, on either tour, of the visitors going over to Britain or Ireland to play even one game. It is my belief that the Four Home Unions should have staged this World Cup without any matches being held in France. When the two losing teams in the French group have completed their matches, they will simply fly home without any involvement on mainland Britain or Ireland. I find that both sad and shaming.

Although the Four Home Unions do host and send separate tours, they also combine as the British Lions and have strong links with each other. France, however, is a much larger country, and has so much interest in the game that it is inconceivable that a World Cup could not have been staged there exclusively. The next time it is the turn of the northern hemisphere, France should have it. Places such as Béziers, Nantes, Lille, Toulon, Toulouse, Narbonne, Perpignan, Tarbes, Lourdes, Biarritz and Nice would provide a magical setting for the tournament. There are splendid stadia in all those centres, too, as well as in a great many others such as Marseilles,

Lyons, Bordeaux and Paris. Even better, most of the matches would be played in a narrow strip across the southern half of a single country, giving every competing team great opportunities to feel a real part of the tournament. A huge banquet could be arranged to welcome every player. I should think half the British Isles and Ireland would take holidays around that time to go to France and enjoy the country, the life and the rugby for a fortnight or so. I cannot imagine a tournament being a greater success anywhere in the world.

As it is, the 1991 World Cup will be spread out far too much. Places where rugby is followed closely, like Bath, Neath, Swansea and Melrose, will not see a single game and that, in my view, is a major error. One of the positive points of the 1987 tournament, despite its failings in other respects, was the fact that you could put on a match like Wales against Canada at Invercargill, on the southern tip of New Zealand's South Island, and get a crowd of around 15,000 locals.

If, as has been suggested, the 1995 World Cup is held in South Africa, there will at last be one country staging the event and I will welcome that arrangement. Never again should we have this mess of spreading it out all over the place, except in the case of the Four Home Unions in Britain and Ireland.

Of course, the first-ever World Cup, in 1987, was ultimately a disaster both for Australia and for me personally. I was blamed for letting a kick from the French left wing, Patrice Lagisquet, bounce late in our semi-final against France at the Concord Oval, and the French picked up the loose ball to go on and score after a bewildering movement involving 11 passes. That aside, throughout the entire tournament I was hardly fit. I had bone scans and X-rays on a troublesome ankle injury but nothing showed up, and I played on in pain with reduced mobility. Three months later, a special scan revealed that I'd been playing with one bone in my ankle split in half. I'd taken pain-killers before each match, but they had had only a limited value. My effectiveness was reduced and, I suppose, looking back, I should not really have played. But I wanted to be out there, and if anyone was to blame for putting me on to the field, then it was me and no one else. It was my decision, and I recognise it now as the wrong one – in fact, it was stupid. But the physios and medical people kept telling me there was only inflammation, so I got on with it as best I could. You cannot communicate to people how much something hurts; they don't really know. When the injury was finally diagnosed, I had to have an operation and missed the Wallabies' tour of Argentina near the end of that year.

We started off that tournament against England in a group match, and although we won, it was a far from impressive display. The chief talking-point was the fact that I was awarded a try which I never touched down properly. It was not a score. If you study the video, it is obvious that I was not happy with the decision the referee made. I looked at him as if to say, 'Well, is it a try or isn't it?' because I knew it wasn't. I was very quiet until he made the decision, and afterwards I told everyone it wasn't a try. It was suggested to me afterwards that I should have caught up with the referee and told him it was no try. While rugby is supposed to stand for honesty and integrity, I have to say that it is very difficult to start telling referees they are wrong during the course of a game, even if it is to your own disadvantage! The referee is there to make the decision and, besides, a lot of other players would not have said anything either in my position. Once the referee has made his decision, reversing it would make him look an idiot. I must admit, however, that if I see the opposition 'score' and know it isn't a try, I get really upset, so maybe I should have said something. But you must consider the circumstances: this was the first game for us in a World Cup everyone in Australia wanted us to win. The pressure was on in every respect, and that pressure dictated attitudes and actions. Like it or not, it is a fact of life. Certain players who have thrown punches and been sent off for doing so would hardly have gone on to the field with such an action in their minds. But the pressure and excitement of the occasion acts as a catalyst, and unpredictable actions result.

England played pretty well in that match, but they didn't make the most of their talent. I had the feeling that they were a bit overwhelmed by Australia, because the previous year we had won the Test series in New Zealand and the Brits know how hard that is to do. Perhaps they took on our reputations rather than us personally, and that is a fatal mistake.

We certainly didn't play crash-hot rugby that day, and as a team we were far from happy with our performance. I don't imagine Alan Jones was too thrilled, either, although he let us calm down afterwards and think about our performances; there were no dramas. But I think we could sense, like the birds feel an oncoming storm, the fact that things were not as they should have been. Alan was starting to blame people, although previously he had always said he would never single out any one individual – and he never had done during our 1984 Grand Slam tour in Britain and Ireland. But now there was more pressure on him to win; that was all it was. Perhaps, too, he felt that his reputation was on the line, although I cannot think why. We had won in Britain in 1984 and again in New Zealand, two years later, and that ought to have been enough to quieten even the fiercest critic of Jonesy. If he didn't see it that way it wouldn't have been surprising: the Australian public and journalists always put a great deal of pressure on all Australian sports teams to win; there can be no room, nor any excuses, for losers in our country.

We followed the England game with matches against the USA and

141

Japan and were pretty hopeless in both. Things had not ignited within the side; we were playing rugby to the standard of our opponents rather than at the level to which we had become accustomed over the previous three years.

Against Ireland in the quarter-finals, though, we put it together very well, and for the first time in the entire tournament we dominated the first half. Then came that momentous semi-final against the French at Concord Oval, a ground hardly beloved of the Wallaby players. Before the start, we knew there were problems. Steve Tuynman pulled out and there was no 'Topo' Rodriguez, who had been a key man in our achievements from 1984 to 1986. Early in the game, we lost Brett Papworth and Bill Campbell through injury. Then Troy Coker won a line-out, but had the ball simply ripped from his grasp by the French lock, Alain Lorieux, who smashed through the front of the line-out to score. What a try to give away.

The reason I did not catch Lagisquet's kick ahead near the end, when the scores were level at 24-24, was that I slipped in the mud trying to reach it. I knew I couldn't get there. But aside from that, it was a great game of rugby, one of the very best in which I have ever played. Sensational things, like brilliant scores, started to happen in that game and we just carried on from there. It was not, in all honesty, our intention to play so open a game, because playing the French in that way can be highly dangerous, as we now know to our cost. But when you are out there, you make decisions and that is how it should be. You cannot rely on the coach all the time. He primes and prepares you, but international players must be able to adapt their thinking to the circumstances in which they find themselves. It's no good looking towards the stand with a 'What do we do now?' expression on your face when things deviate from what has been expected.

Running the ball very nearly beat the French that day, so I don't think our tactics can be criticised heavily. In the end, an extraordinary try, which was made possible because the French players refused to let the movement die, won the match. But at the end of a pulsating game there was only one score between the sides, a fact which confirmed our quality. It was a desperately near miss for us, and I believe it should be consigned to history as purely that, rather than as some sort of watershed for Australian rugby just because we happened to be on the wrong end of the scoreline. Reverses occur, and you can only shrug, accept it and hope luck favours you next time. I don't hold with the view that just because you lose one match it's the end of the world.

Nor, in this case, should that Wallaby side be condemned because of its failure to win the World Cup. It had triumphed magnificently against every rugby-playing nation of the world, South Africa excluded. Every Test, every conceivable contest had been put before us and we had shown ourselves to be one of *the* great teams in the history of the game. Not only that, but we had done so with a flair, a style and a spring in our step which made watching us compelling entertainment. Look at the crowds in Britain and Ireland, and in New Zealand, when we went there. Had the World Cup matches been played at the Sydney Cricket Ground, there would have been marvellous attendances in Sydney, too.

The only criticism I do have of our side at that time (and since) is that we tended to spend the first 60 minutes of a match kicking the ball and then running it in the final 20 minutes. That I never understood. It didn't happen in the World Cup semi-final because we were sucked into a running contest almost from the off. But that was not the norm, by any means. I suppose most would say that this is a practical, pragmatic approach suited to the modern-day game. But as a player who yearns to see the ball moved (I hope in my direction more than once or twice in a match), I don't go down that road. I would like to see teams being brave enough to move the ball around the paddock whenever they are in a promising position. Just look back to the 1990 soccer World Cup, when teams would not attack each other. There were fewer goals scored in that tournament than in any previous World Cup finals because teams were scared of attack. We don't want rugby to become like that.

To me, there is no crazier sight in the game than a team which has played dull, predictable rugby based on kicking for three-quarters of a game suddenly throwing the ball around the field as though it were a hot potato. What they are doing is throwing away their principles, too, because if you believe in a kicking game, then adhere to that. Don't just switch to a totally different style only because you are behind and in trouble. What sort of a playing policy is that? Besides, if you suddenly start running the ball late in a game in which you have kicked the thing all afternoon, the opposition will be encouraged. They know that they have got you and that you are desperate. They will feel you are bound to make mistakes and they'll probably be right. And they'll be sure to win.

New Zealand never displayed such tactical naïveté during that 1987 World Cup. They adhered rigidly to their game plan from the very start and imposed themselves on opponents. They needed to fit in a new hooker because Andy Dalton was not fit, and David Kirk became the replacement captain. But that was it; no other changes in personnel or plans. And I always felt that that was the best thing they could have done: to keep their team and play. Granted, they were not a particularly enterprising New Zealand team because they just did what All Black teams normally do. But they had many good players, and the right side won the tournament, there are no arguments about that. France had expended all their energy in beating us in the semi-final – perhaps they regarded that match as their 'final' rather than the one against New Zealand. Personally, I think we would have given the All Blacks a much tougher final. The way they were playing, though, I don't believe we would have beaten them. There was a rhythm, a purring consistency and inevitability about their ultimate triumph.

The chief lesson that should have been learned from that World Cup, but wasn't, was that future tournaments should be held in one country. New Zealand, for example, would easily sustain enough interest and support to put on the entire tournament at some stage in the future. From the northern tip of North Island to Invercargill at the foot of the South Island, interest in the game is consistent. Crowds would swell if the event were being held exclusively in that country. Another lesson which ought to have been carefully digested was the fact that some players had to go home too quickly after they had lost, I suppose just to save the authorities some money. I had a lot of friends in the Italian team but I never saw them once because they were based in New Zealand and had to fly home the day after they lost. That is ridiculous.

All the teams should stay in one hotel prior to the start of the tournament so that a grand opening ceremony can be held and all the players can meet up and spend time together at some point. Then you could disperse to your various regional headquarters, where you would play your matches. But you would at least have had one grand dinner together where you could meet guys from all over the world and make friends.

The 1991 World Cup was destined to be a huge event in every sense: commercial, rugby, travel, media coverage, the lot. But as regards matters on the field, at the time of writing I sense that unless we can beat them, it is simply going to be a question of who will meet New Zealand in the final. Assessing the form at this stage, and given the fact that they have the ludicrous advantage of being able to play every match on their home ground, you would have to say Scotland look as well placed as anyone to reach the final. I'm not quite sure how it can be that in a tournament being staged in five countries, one nation has the advantage of being able to play every single match in its home city, Edinburgh. It's a pretty daft situation because it will give the Scots every possibility of just one journey, to Twickenham for the final.

As the groups are arranged, it looks as though Australia might meet the All Blacks in one of the semi-finals, assuming both teams do not slip up in the group matches. If we should clash in the semi-final, I cannot think of a better place than Lansdowne Road, Dublin, at which to meet. Whoever wins and loses, I predict some party (or wake) afterwards.

My hope for the 1991 tournament is that things do not follow the predicted pattern. It would be nice to think that one highly-fancied nation might encounter some unexpectedly tough opposition and find pitfalls along the road. It would be good to see some of the so-called lesser nations, such as Japan or Western Samoa, coming through to achieve a major surprise (just as long as it's not against us!). And I hope that all the quarter-finals and both semi-finals are closely contested matches which go right to the wire. The semi-final between New Zealand and Wales held in Brisbane in 1987 was a farce, it was so one-sided. Let's hope that does not happen again.

People made much of the New Zealanders losing four players to Rugby League in 1990 but the only key defector was John Gallagher. The others were not even in the All Black side. So, believe me, New Zealand will still be very good at the 1991 World Cup. They have formed a new midfield pairing of Craig Innes and Walter Little, both of whom look outstandingly promising young players to me. That is New Zealand's way: they lose someone apparently essential and someone else steps into the breach. That, conversely, is Australia's problem.

Unless Australia develops a lot of high-quality players by October 1991, I am not certain we will have the back-up to get to the final. For example, if you discount Michael Lynagh, there is no world-class, experienced five-eighth in Australia. Maybe David Knox of Randwick and New South Wales could do the job, although up until 1989 he was playing full-back for Randwick.

A small matter it may be, but I was concerned by the talk of some of the Australian players in the 1990 season. The World Cup dominated thinking in some people's minds, even before we had played our 1989 Test series against France or embarked on the tour of New Zealand at the end of our domestic season. That was ridiculous. I have never subscribed to the view that everything should be thrown overboard to prepare for the next World Cup. If all you think about is next year, then you are not putting your complete energies into what is happening now. It is a pointless exercise, anyway, because there is always the very real possibility that injury will interrupt someone's career and force him out of a series or a particular tournament.

France, whom we met and beat 2-1 in a series in Australia in 1990, are the great unpredictables of the world game. They played poorly at times, both in our tour to France in 1989 (the Tests were drawn 1-1) and then in Australia. Then they exposed our unjustified confidence by not only beating us in the final Test at Sydney on the last day of June 1990, but also producing some splendid, running rugby which gave the lie to the theory that Jacques Fouroux, then their coach, would never permit a flowing, expansive game. They scored two fine tries and ran the ball at times from deep in their own half, just like the French sides of the past. But when they went home and met the All Blacks in a Test series at the end of the year, they lost both matches and saw Jacques Fouroux resign as coach. That surprised me, for I believed that Fouroux would have got them together as a credible force in time for the World Cup. People criticise him, but look at France's record during the 1980s when he was in charge – they dominated the Five Nations Championship for virtually the entire decade. Now that he has gone, I have no idea what they will be like. Nor, I suspect, do they have a clue.

I spent four days in France near the end of last year visiting Lloyd Walker and Michael Checker (both Randwick players), who were playing for Castres in the French Championship. I was disturbed to see in the club match I watched live and also in the club games I saw on television that running rugby seemed to have died in France. Only the boot of the No 10 seemed to matter. And yet, as I have said, the national team played some great running rugby against us in 1990 and looked to be trying to produce open, positive play in the 1991 Five Nations Championship. Daniel Dubroca, who took over from Fouroux, is a likeable guy; I met him a few times during the French tour last year and enjoyed chatting with him. But he has very limited coaching experience and faces a hard task to pull together a new team in his own style. These things take time, years in most cases, and time was not on the side of the French for the World Cup. If you take out France as genuine contenders to win the World Cup, you are left with only two countries, England and Scotland, to challenge the All Blacks. There is no one else, except of course the Wallabies.

England look a potent force but the only thing that puzzles me about them is that, for two years in succession, they blew outstanding chances of winning the Five Nations Championship. You can detect quite early the great sides in the world game: they show a steady rise and, more essentially, an ability to front up, to emerge when the going is toughest. The All Blacks have done it for years; the Wallabies did it in the Alan Jones era. They come to a crunch game, perhaps a difficult one on paper, and their high level of skill and self-belief sees them through. But in the case of England, having climbed on to the pedestal, they then fell right off it two years running. That suggests there is a flaw in their make-up.

Whether it was due to the coaches being no good when the heat was really on, or the players not really wanting deep down to win, or an inability on the part of the players to retain their concentration, I do not know. But they made an absolute mess of winning in Cardiff in 1989 against a terribly ordinary Welsh team, and they fell to another technically inferior side, Scotland, when the two teams met to decide the 1990 Grand Slam and Five Nations Championship title in Edinburgh, last year. If I were a Pom, I'd be disturbed at that trend. It is all right to suffer the odd defeat; that happens. Australia, remember, lost the second Test to New Zealand in Dunedin in

1986, but we then got it right and won the next, when the pressure was really on, to take the series. From the evidence available, it seems that England may lack the capacity to handle the pressure of expectation at the highest level. And if that is true, then they will never realise their considerable potential as a side.

Ever since they beat us at Twickenham in 1988, I have felt that English rugby has been on a considerable 'up'. They lost the 1989 Five Nations title only because of that defeat in Wales and in 1990 they played some fine rugby to thrash France in Paris and Wales and Ireland at Twickenham. Scotland, who had struggled all season, should not have been good enough to deny England even at Murrayfield, but at the crux, England failed. Maybe that will happen again in the future. I had the distinct feeling that the Poms panicked against Scotland. Admittedly, the referee that day, David Bishop of New Zealand, did a very bad job and it is perfectly possible that with a referee such as Norling, England would have won. Scotland got away with collapsed scrums right on their own line and were offside throughout the match. But having said all that, you have to overcome such difficulties and have the confidence to keep going. The great sides surmount those problems and emerge triumphant at the end.

However, their Grand Slam success of 1991 leads me to believe that England have now learned how to win. The fact that they blew it two years running meant that they were ready to explode. They did that in the 1991 Championship, although to win the Grand Slam they had to drop most of their free-flowing rugby of the previous season, which was a pity. But the way they played indicated to me that they were a side desperate to win a title. They had learned the lessons of their two failures and were determined not to lose a third time. They kept it tighter and played a pretty professional game. The confidence gained from becoming European champions was to be a major bonus going into the World Cup. But a word of warning to them: they will have to revert to using their threequarters much more if they want to win the World Cup. You don't beat the best teams in the world by playing ten-man rugby.

England will surely have a very solid, experienced pack of forwards for the World Cup. The back row should be excellent with players of great strength in Richards and Hall and the locks, Dooley and Ackford, gave the Lions plenty of problems on their 1989 tour. Probyn is no spring chicken at tight-head prop, but if the rest of them are mobile enough, they may be able to get away with having him there. It is probably a good idea to have brought in a younger prop, Leonard, on the loose head for Rendall, at 36, was getting too old. In my view, England need a full-back, too. What clouds that particular issue is the fact that the guy they have now, Hodgkinson, is a world-class goal-kicker so I expect they will stick with him. But I don't think he is international class as a player.

The attitude in English rugby has certainly changed. It was refreshing – and surprising – to see teams running the ball at us when we toured England in 1988. The standard in the provinces was, I thought, quite good at that time. There is no doubt that England have the capacity to be a great team if they really want to be. Deep-seated confidence is lacking, but if they add that, then they will be a damned hard side to beat. But you only acquire that by regular victories and, more critically, winning titles and trophies.

In the wake of their 1990 Grand Slam, Scotland could be the dark horses, not just to do well in the World Cup but perhaps to win it. Ask them to produce 25 or 30 world-class players like New Zealand, or even England, and they could not hope to do it. But they seem able to find 16 or so high-quality performers whom they can integrate into their team and make into extremely competent players who do well within the system they employ. And that is the secret: you can choose the best 15 players in the world, but if they don't gel and fit into the game plan you want to play, then they will not be the force you imagine. Scotland are also very well coached and have clearly benefited from consistent policy in choosing coaches. One has faded out and another, groomed some years earlier within the system, has stepped up to take his place. They don't go casting around the lakes and highlands for some total stranger; there always seems to be someone inside the camp, who knows exactly how things operate, to take charge. That, of course, is the way of Liverpool Football club, and look at the success they have enjoyed at the top of the English game. Randwick, too, benefited from the fact that when Bob Dwyer finished as coach Jeff Sayle, a Randwick club man through and through, took his place. 'Sayler' understood the history, the make-up and traditions of the club; he brought a continuity in playing pattern and style which ensured our continuing success.

Scotland will have enhanced their confidence by what they achieved on their 1990 tour of New Zealand. True, they did not beat the All Blacks, but they gave them enough to think about in both Tests to show what they could do given a British crowd behind them. Scotland would be my choice to go very close to the World Cup because of the advantage of the draw. England, unless they beat New Zealand to finish top of their group, look as though they might have to go to Paris to meet France in the quarter-final, and that wouldn't be an easy game. France, whatever their past problems, always have the capacity to pick a team and see it perform exhilaratingly. That is the chief danger they present; they are always capable of beating anyone because their club structure is so strong. Even in the midst of their worst troubles at international level, it is undeniable that club rugby in France is powerful.

Of the other Home Union sides, I cannot, with the best will in the world, see Wales or Ireland threatening to win the World Cup. I must be careful here what I say, because we meet Wales in our group and the match at Cardiff will be a tough one. Besides, I have some sympathy for Wales because they have been drained, as Australian rugby has been drained, by so many defections to Rugby League. How can you expect any side to play consistently outstanding, winning rugby if over the years it has lost players in the kind of numbers which have deserted the Welsh national side. I know of some, and the list makes pretty formidable reading: Jonathan Davies, Jonathan Griffiths and Gary Pearce (Llanelli); Allan Bateman, Rowland Phillips and Mark Jones (Neath); Paul Moriarty and Stuart Evans (Swansea); Kevin Ellis (Bridgend); Terry Holmes, David Young and Adrian Hadley (Cardiff); Robert Ackerman (London Welsh); David Bishop (Pontypool) and John Devereux (Bridgend). There are others, too.

Wales was once an absolute hotbed of rugby, a place whose reputation almost made you afraid to go there. But no longer. That Wales' national side lost to a Barbarians team of which I was a member in 1990, when all we in the Barbarians wanted to do was go out, throw the ball around and have some fun, was an indictment of the depths to which the Welsh game has fallen. They should have skinned us for our cavalier approach, yet we won a game we were hardly trying to win. That must have been a shattering blow for Welsh rugby.

Ireland, too, have had their problems in recent times. The decision to rebuild their side in the middle of the 1990-91 season was a bold one, but was probably prompted by the result against the touring Argentinians at the end of October. Ireland were desperately lucky to win in the seventh minute of injury-time through a Michael Kiernan penalty goal. England and Scotland quickly proved what a shocking result that was for Ireland by annihilating Argentina soon afterwards.

However, by the time the Five Nations Championship ended in March, Ireland were playing some thrilling rugby. They had a virtually new team but had made rapid progress in a very short time. The backs were getting the ball and using it intelligently. They looked pretty quick to me, too, and players like Simon Geoghegan, Jim Staples and Rob Saunders had come in and had a dazzling effect. But, just when they seemed on course for better things, five-eighth Brian Smith signed for Balmain Rugby League club. I have to be honest: I don't believe Ireland should ever have chosen Smith in the first place, as I said earlier. He wasn't born in the country, he did not even live in Ireland, and he just flew in for big games. It would be like Australia choosing a New Zealander to play for the Wallabies, something I would find appalling. And after all the fuss, Smith walked out only days after apparently promising Irish officials that he would stay for the

World Cup. I reckon they are better off without him.

I believe Ireland's policy was right – find good young players if the old guard is ailing. They have clearly identified that problem, and by unearthing these talented youngsters they have shown that such new blood exists. It took a crisis to force the change, but now things look brighter.

It seems to me, watching as often as I have been able to from Italy, that there are two levels nowadays in European rugby. England, Scotland and France occupy the top level; Ireland, Wales, Romania and Italy the lower level. England, of course, always should be in that upper echelon because they have literally thousands of players from which to choose. It is in fact a shocking comment on previous English administrations that they have been unable to achieve success for their country given such a huge depth of playing talent. Without doubt, England could and should have been a good side years ago but, for a variety of reasons, they have clearly failed to achieve.

Scotland won a Grand Slam in 1984 and did it again in 1990. Wales have had many barren years, save for an isolated Triple Crown in 1988. Ireland had their problems during the 1980s but still have an infinitely superior record to England's during the decade. But the signs are that England should go on to develop a very useful side for the future and especially for the World Cup. Whether Scotland can mask their comparatively limited number of players remains to be seen, but the Scots are a canny lot, and I wouldn't bet against them.

At the end of the day, I always feel that Australia and New Zealand can usually beat the Five Nations teams. That is because we have the capacity to have a go, to attack from deep and to do the unpredictable. Too often, British and Irish teams are far too orthodox; you know almost exactly what they are going to do. But the Wallabies, although perhaps lapsing into the same trend too much in recent years, still possess the ability to do the unexpected. And we show it at times. That is why we have had so much success against the Home Unions in recent years, the odd defeat excepted.

I would love to get through to the World Cup final with Australia by beating the All Blacks in the semi-final. It would be a wonderful boost for Australian rugby and confirmation that we always possess the capability to take them on and defeat them, perhaps more so than almost any other country. And the nation I'd like us to meet in the final? I couldn't really care less, as long as we get there. But maybe England, because they are playing some good rugby. Their backs look impressive, and two teams trying to move the ball would make a magnificent spectacle for the World Cup final. An Ashes Test for the World Cup – that sounds suitably dramatic to me. The meeting of the two old enemies could produce some sensational rugby football to present on the world stage.

CHAPTER
—11—

FIVE NATIONS FARE

When the Italian rugby season was in mid-winter hibernation for a couple of
weeks around the middle of February 1990, I decided to make a short visit
to Britain. One of the delights of the game in Italy is the fact that there are
these little breaks in the season's programme. That year, we had a week or
ten days off at that time, and later on another free week at the end of
November. I strongly recommend such an arrangement to anyone organising
the game at the highest level: it offers all the players the opportunity to
recover from any niggling injuries, to retain their physical and mental
stamina and to remain keen and eager for the games.

The climate I encountered in Britain was not quite to an Australian's
liking: wet, cold, damp and drizzly. It became increasingly hard to picture
guys out surfing at Manly beach, or the Queenslanders steaming gently in
their sauna of a climate! But to be fair, there were compensations: a blazing
log fire at a Kent village pub where I went one night for dinner, and a warm
Edinburgh restaurant where I found myself eating later in the week. To see
and experience such things is an attraction for guys like myself. When you
tour, you spend so much time rushing from one venue to the next that you
miss out on a lot of very pleasant places to see and spend some time in. The
pressure-cooker atmosphere of a rugby tour is never-ending, and the
minute it is finished, you are on the plane home. There is no time to do the
kind of things which ought to form an important part of a tour.

I flew to Edinburgh as a very interested observer at the first Five
Nations Championship match I had ever attended. Just in case any southern
hemisphere readers are not familiar with the reputation of the Five Nations
Championship, let me say that it is the highlight of the winter in northern

hemisphere rugby. A yearly event comprising the rugby-playing countries of England, Scotland, Wales, Ireland and France, it has become, in many respects, as much of a social season from January to March as a rugby tournament.

In Edinburgh, the famous Princes Street is thronged with supporters from the two nations on the Saturday morning before the game. There is a buzz in the streets; rugby is the topic of conversation wherever you go. I am told that when there is a big match on the major stores announce the result over their tannoy systems. What interest!

Go to Twickenham for any international at that time of year and you will see the English classes associated with the game at play. Believe me, it's some sight! The Rolls-Royces and Jaguar cars are parked early in the huge car-park at Twickenham, and the picnic hampers are opened in the boot. I suppose it's really only the equivalent of a barbie at Brisbane, but you'd have to say these jokers have the organisation and quality down to a fine art. Bottles of claret clink in the back, filled glasses standing between huge chunks of game pie or slices of smoked salmon. They seem to put anything they can shoot into the pies: pheasant, pigeon, partridge, the lot. It must be a hell of a time of year for the wildlife of Great Britain!

They tell me the 'picnic' – some picnic – usually ends with a good cognac, to fortify everyone for 80 minutes in the cold and wet. Then it's on with the duffle coats and into the expensive seats at the ground. And afterwards there is more of the same, and probably champagne (especially if England have won). It's a world away from Randwick or Manly Oval before a Saturday match!

The one thing all the major venues for the Championship matches (Twickenham, Cardiff, Edinburgh, Dublin and Paris) have in common is the sense of special occasion when the Five Nations Championship circus is in town. People have told me that Parc des Princes for a France-Australia Test match bears little resemblance to the same venue for a game in the Championship. I suppose all the thousands of visiting fans, who regard Paris as the favoured venue for a rugby weekend, make it special. Without doubt, it's a great sight to see all the fans travelling the length and breadth of the British Isles, Ireland and to Paris to support their teams.

The atmosphere created by those supporters at the stadia is fantastic, too, if Murrayfield on 17 February 1990 was any indication. Scotland versus France was the match I attended, and I found it an extremely interesting experience. I looked at the big ground filled with supporters, around 50,000 I suppose, and thought how wonderful it would be to play in front of such a crowd at every home game. They never seem to have any difficulty selling tickets for Five Nations Championship games. In fact, for the big games such as England versus Wales and Scotland versus France, you could probably sell another 30,000 tickets without any problem, if only you had the space to fit them all in. On that score, it surprises me that no one in Britain or Ireland has built a ground capable of holding 100,000 people. Even if they filled that only twice a year, the money raised would probably be enough to pay off the loans needed to finance such a stadium. There is such a scramble for tickets for these games that I find it odd that no one has sanctioned a really big ground. I know that Twickenham's capacity will be around 72,000 when the building work is finished, but even that number will not cater for all those who want to watch the internationals.

As an Australian player, I would regard it as fabulous to have the kind of atmosphere generated by the 50,000 voices I heard at Murrayfield last year transported to Australia for all our home games. The trouble there is that if you play a team like New Zealand, half the support in the 40,000-capacity Sydney Football Stadium is cheering for the visiting team. In 1989, when Australia met the British Lions, there were thousands of British supporters in the ground. At Edinburgh last year, I could only drool at the volume of support for the home team. When Scotland attacked, there was a great roar such as you might hear from water at Niagara Falls. Very intimidating for the away team, and wonderfully encouraging for the home side.

However, having found the atmosphere itself highly invigorating, bracing even, I have to say I didn't think the rugby itself was crash-hot. From watching this match live and assorted others on television in Italy, I formed the impression that teams seem to apply a lot of pressure in the Five Nations Championship games but find it difficult to put points on the board. And when it comes to scoring tries, many teams seem to be really short on tactics. There appeared to be a common reliance on the forward bulldozer approach, and if that did not work, several of the sides seemed stymied for another route to success. Apart, that is, from the ubiquitous goal-kicking. That goes on whatever the changing trends in the world game, and I suppose nations in the southern hemisphere regard it as just as important as those in Europe. Would New Zealand have won so many matches since 1987 without Grant Fox in their side? I somehow doubt it. And there is no disputing the fact that Michael Lynagh has won Australia several matches which we might otherwise have lost.

However, within the confines of the Five Nations Championship, there exists an attitude of win at all costs, regardless of style or approach. Piling more points on to the board than your opponents is the sole objective in this particular competition. At Edinburgh, France had a team which contained some of the finest backs in the world: Serge Blanco, Patrice Lagisquet, Philippe Sella and Frank Mesnel. Yet those guys hardly touched the ball because the forwards seemed content to fight a war of attrition up front. The idea of allowing the ball to escape or working primarily to set up the guys behind the scrum did not seem to occur to the French forwards. I found that extraordinary. Of course, no back line in the world is going to thank you for shovelling out poor quality ball, but the French had plenty of chances to release a fast, penetrative back line and yet the will to do it simply did not exist. I found that baffling.

What ball the French did secure was booted away by Camberabero, which was symptomatic of the ills of the modern-day game. Where once there was an elegant piece of running, today a clinical boot is applied to the ball. The freedom for which the game was once renowned has now become so contracted as to be negligible at times. This is a disturbing trend. Even a great deal of the kicking is of poor quality. I can perhaps understand it when teams are on their own 22 and under heavy pressure. You want to get away from the danger zone and work your way upfield, although my previously-stated views that it is often easier to make progress by running the ball rather than kicking it still hold good. Never miss the opportunity to attack from any position on the field.

I see teams these days kicking the ball when they have won possession on their opponents' 22-metre line. That is crazy. Guys are kicking the ball simply for the sake of it or, more usually, because they are simply not good enough to make scores by creative play with the ball in their own hands. They are inferior players. Kicking the ball has become the soft option; it means the blame can be apportioned elsewhere if the attacking team fails to score. Those who cannot break the defence by running the ball or setting up their back line should not be on the field in the first place. They kick because there is nothing else they can do.

While I have the hatchet in my hands, let me wield it, too, in the direction of the coaches. Because, ultimately, these are the guys who decide on the tactics. A half-back or first five-eighth cannot kick the ball all day long unless the coach has sanctioned such a ploy. Don't tell me that international players don't go on to the field without clear tactics laid down for them by their respective coaches. The game has become too professional, too well-planned for that not to be the case. So if you see a guy kicking the leather off the ball, you can invariably bet that the guy behind the tactic is the coach, an anonymous face in the crowd but the one responsible for the fact that everybody is being bored to tears.

I would not argue that coaches should not play to their strengths. But it is my view that they also have a duty towards those thousands of people who pay to go and see a game of rugby as well as to the millions of others at home watching it on television. You cannot say 'To hell with those people'; they must be offered something by way of an attraction in the game. I'll tell you this much – if the game and its coaches always ignore the wishes of the spectators they are heading down a pretty dark alley, because countless numbers of supporters will be lost along the way.

The trouble with putting pre-programmed players on to any sports field, whether it is a rugby international or a club tennis match, is that if the players are stuffed full of advice like turkeys at Christmas, then they are going to play like – well, turkeys! They will not know what to do when the moment comes for making a decision of their own. The best coaches are the ones who say to you, 'It will be you who will be out there presented with the opportunities. You have to decide in each situation; think about the decision-making process both on the field and before you go out there. It's up to you'. A coach can guide, offer advice and encouragement; he can cajole, berate and sympathise. But he can never, ever be the one to make the decisions when they matter, on the field during the game. That being so, isn't it better for the players to get used to handling this aspect of the game as soon as they possibly can?

At Edinburgh, I formed the opinion that not too much thought on the part of the players was going into what I was seeing. It appeared that some very formal guidelines were being followed. I waited in vain for someone to decide that a change in tactics was required. Once the pattern had become established, you could have closed your eyes for 20 minutes and found exactly the same style in front of you when you opened them again. Scotland, I felt, were offside far, far too often. Their fly-half, Craig Chalmers would put up a bomb above the French full-back and Finlay Calder, the Scottish flanker, would be first there, even if the kick had been launched 40 yards back. I'm the first to say that Calder was a good player, but in his final season in the Five Nations Championship, which this was, I do not believe he was the greyhound he appeared to be, judging from his presence in some of those situations. I watched him closely a couple of times after that and my suspicions were confirmed – he was fringing in front of the kicker, and getting there first from an offside position. It was all done very quietly and most shrewdly but, at the end of the day, it was illegal.

Of course, it is desperately hard for referees to detect this, particularly if the player is one who emerges from the melee of players and is just a few yards over the gain line. The official is bound to be following the ball, so he would need eyes in the back of his head to detect someone stealing five or even ten yards behind him. Furthermore, it is my belief that certain teams are aware of the fact that if they persist with a particular technical offence, such as offside, they are likely to get away with it more often than not. They work on the philosophy that if a referee really did pick them up every single time he saw them committing an offence, he would be blowing his whistle for the whole match. This, quite obviously, would be totally unacceptable because the game would never flow and one side would claim it had been refereed out of the contest. The referee's name would be mud and he might never get another international match.

All this, of course, is known well enough by the coaches and managers of the national sides. It is especially relevant when a referee is from the other side of the world, and is perhaps particularly nervous about handling a big pressure game in the European Five Nations Championship. He is therefore likely to be more tolerant than some others from Europe who are better used to the occasion. It seems to me that some teams nowadays go out to play the referee almost as much as the opposition. They try him out, see what he is sharp on and where he is more lax, and then they try to exploit the latter accordingly.

Take offside, for example. A referee who has picked up a team two or three times in the space of five minutes is going to put himself under some fairly heavy pressure from the home crowd. Every player in the home team is more than aware of that. It will influence his action if he faces a decision on whether or not to go offside a couple of minutes later. If he does, the chances are that most referees will think they have blown their whistle enough in the preceding few minutes and ignore it. That is where Scotland are so clever, because they play on that fact. They know that, by the law of averages, no referee will go on penalising the players from the same team. And if, say, almost every forward in a certain team is prepared to hang around offside, the referee will be able to do little about it.

If one guy in particular stands out as being offside, then it is easier for a referee. He can be warned twice, and then, if he persists, sent off. But what does the referee do if it is always a different player? You cannot warn a player if he has been caught offside twice in a 15- or 20-minute period, that would be absurd. But if every one of his forward colleagues has also been offside twice in that time-span, the team could have committed 16 offside offences in 20 minutes. See my point? At the end of it, the referee could not take one guy aside and deliver an official warning, not for just two offences. He would probably claim that they were technical offences without malicious intent. That argument would certainly hold up in law. But I wonder whether malicious intent is always missing among the teams who do work out how to play referees with such care and planning.

One thing is certain: at Murrayfield that particular day, from my seat in the press box high up at the back of the main stand, I found it impossible to see who the good players were. There were 30 players trying to play rugby (29 after the Frenchman Alain Carminati had been sent off), but not one stood out. The pattern seemed interminable; scrum or line-out followed by a kick, either to touch or up above the defence. If variety is the spice of life, as it is claimed, then a very plain, stodgy menu was set before us that day. Even France wouldn't attack; they, too, seemed influenced by this mania.

Scotland won the match 21-0, but until Carminati's dismissal they held only a slender 3-0 lead, having had the wind advantage before half-time. I have to say that it was far from riveting entertainment. Scotland went on to win the Grand Slam that season, but they did not look a great side to me. Gavin Hastings ran cross-field 20 yards and forward five yards, Craig Chalmers kicked the ball, usually just up in the air for everyone to chase after, but Scott Hastings did well with very limited opportunities. What disappointed me about Scotland was the fact that their players didn't seem to want to try anything a bit different. The only reason I could come up with for this sorry state of affairs was a fear of what their coaches might say if they departed from the pre-ordained plan. And, if that is so, it is appalling.

The fear of losing, and of trying something different, has infiltrated Five Nations Championship rugby. I suppose nations are aware that in recent years they have been able to play dull, low-risk, percentage rugby against France and get away with it, whereas years ago they would not have survived. French magic would have conjured something out of nothing to defeat all that dross. Against the teams in the British Isles and Ireland, I suppose Scotland have proved, by their 1990 Grand Slam win, that they can get away with this kind of limited rugby and still triumph, if that is the appropriate word. But such a dull style would not be enough against teams like the All Blacks or Australia. The Wallabies played Scotland twice in four years on their last two tours to Britain and flogged them each time by over 30 points – 37-12 in 1984 and 32-13 in 1988. That was not a coincidence. The reason is that the way Scotland play doesn't go anywhere against a really good team. You can squeeze through in a dog-fight such as the Grand Slam decider against England at Murrayfield in March 1990, but in other circumstances, against a team with a different philosophy, it will not be good enough. This much must have been apparent when Scotland went to New Zealand in June 1990 for a tour which included two Test matches.

Despite good spells in each Test, Scotland failed both times, losing 31-16 at Dunedin and, admittedly in a much tighter game, 21-18 at Eden Park, Auckland. Scotland, to my mind, need a few different ideas and more inventiveness generally in their play. They ought to try to move the ball around far more to utilise their strong runners outside the scrum such as the Hastings brothers and Tony Stanger. They ought to be trying to make the opposition think more about what they are going to do, rather than just presenting them with kicks ahead. Just because they beat England in that Grand Slam match it does not mean they are the finished product as a side. Not by any means.

I am quite sure I will stir up a hornet's nest of disagreement by saying this, but I found England a much more enterprising side than the Scots in the 1990 Championship, Grand Slam defeat notwithstanding. England had some very decent backs available to them, and they seemed prepared to use that talent, rather than to choose it and then leave it shivering with cold while the forwards hogged the ball. That was the story for years, but now England appear to have a pattern of play. Carling takes it up and the forwards pile in to secure second-phase ball, which they seek to move fast. And it is not only guys like Jeremy Guscott, Will Carling and Rory Underwood who have impressed me; it seems to me that quite recently, for the first time, the English pack has really been determined to get around the field rather than moving from set piece to set piece.

England showed they could be a force in world rugby by their performances in 1990 and 1991. And I believe they have far more potential than the Scots because their players are of a better quality and seem more willing to try more options. Their backs stay on their feet much better now, which is a great bonus, and of course Carling is especially good at that. And now that their forwards get there quickly, all kinds of possibilities are being opened up for the team.

I always counsel patience as the key. Someone once told me to take my time in scoring situations, and that advice has proved useful. Perhaps England still panic a little in such circumstances, but as their side settles down together that fault should be eliminated. England perform the basics very well indeed. They have excellent presence in the line-outs, the way they drive is superb and the scrum is big and solid. They seem to have moved away from the days when their forwards were big lumbering guys who ran out of steam if they moved around the field for half-an-hour! When they use it, England's policy of running the ball is full of wisdom. If you have guys like Guscott and Underwood available further out, why on earth kick it? I felt that in the 1990 Five Nations Championship the running game was still alien to a few of the English players. A couple of the guys were not quite certain what they were supposed to be doing. The play of Guscott against Wales, when he lost what should have been several more scoring opportunities through poorly-timed passes and wayward distribution of the ball, was a classic example.

Guscott could be a very good player if he had a bit more confidence in his ability. He also has to learn to think not only for himself and what he can achieve. I've seen him play in matches where it has been obvious that he has passed only when there has been nothing on for him. That's not true team play: he has to learn all the options available in a situation and start selecting the correct one. The word in the game is that he may be worried about taking the hard knocks. I don't know whether that is true or not – we heard it in the match between the Barbarians and New Zealand in 1989 at Twickenham. One of the All Blacks punched him early on and that was it, little was seen of him afterwards. He has to learn to play on and cope with all that. In international rugby you have got to cop it at times. It might look attractive and wonderfully glamorous from a comfortable seat in the grandstand, but out on the field there is nothing glamorous about being caught at the bottom of a ruck and feeling boots driving into your body. But that's the game and you must accept that side of it.

England's players must try to think the same way as each other and they must persevere. With their playing pattern, they will be successful if they can scale the psychological barrier which has prevented them from winning honours so far. It is my firm belief that England will iron out these few faults and emerge as a very fine side indeed. The organisation and aggression, so often key factors which have been missing in recent England sides, is there in abundance now. They look like a team which wants to win and knows it can. But their problem in the past has been that they have wasted the ball won by the forwards. That fault is only eliminated when players know what they are going to do and are confident enough to make the decisions on the field. This goes back to what I was saying earlier in this chapter.

England can still get a great deal more out of their backs because they now have a scrum-half, Richard Hill, who has transformed their play at half-back. Hill has made a vast difference to the entire England side because he has been able to give Rob Andrew those extra couple of seconds as well as good-quality ball. He happily drives on the average-quality possession with the help of his forwards, and he has the physical presence to do it successfully. But when he does release it, Andrew gets quality ball with space and time. It is no wonder he has improved so much.

This is one area in which I disagree strongly with the tactics of the former French coach Jacques Fouroux. His ploy of using the half-back to throw in and the hooker to act as scrum-half to take the line-out ball and drive it on denies the options of speed out wide and surprise to the team. My view is that if you win quick ball you should release it straight away and give the first five-eighth that extra bit of time to decide on something. Then it comes down to a contest of skill and cunning behind the scrum between the opposing sets of backs. But just driving the ball back into the forwards from a line-out, which is what the French have been doing in recent years, is a waste of fast possession.

People have said to me at various times that they suppose it is now virtually impossible to score tries from first-phase, set-piece possession. I regard such talk as that of the inferior player or the person who just does not understand the game. Of course it is possible to score tries from the first phase. After all, the best teams have always done it, and the great sides continue to do it to this day. Maybe defences are better organised nowadays, perhaps players are fitter, which enables them to cover better and longer in matches, and I am equally sure that greater skill and craft is required to break through the best defences. But don't tell me it still cannot be done, because even to say that is an admission of poor technique.

Some teams seem to think that it is only when you start to get second- or third-phase ball that you can score tries, because it is only then that defences are disorganised and broken. Show me a side which takes that viewpoint and I'll show you a lousy, unsuccessful rugby team. In this game, like any other, you must have complete belief in your own ability and that of your colleagues to score the points that win games. Not just by goal-kicking, either, but by opening up defences and scoring tries. That is the essence of the entire game. To accept defeat in its most fundamental task, the scoring of tries, suggests an inferior character and an inferior talent.

England are guilty of neither. Their performances in 1990 against France and Wales were excellent, and even in the Grand Slam game against the Scots they scored a great try. But playing as a unit is the most important thing in international rugby, and I am sure all the countries competing in the Five Nations Championship are aware of that fact. Australia should consider it, too, because that is what we lacked during 1989 and 1990. We were not working hard enough on those aspects, either.

I enjoyed my visit to Edinburgh. I found it a strange experience to go to a Test match and sit around before the start, chatting to some old friends and acquaintances. My inner self wanted to go down to the dressing-room, get ready and think about the game. He couldn't understand I was having a day off from the action! It was fun to get out on the Friday evening and taste some Scottish food and get a flavour, too, of the atmosphere in the city the night before a game. When you play, you tend to lead a very sheltered, protected existence, well away from all the distractions. That is how it should be, but it was interesting to see things from the other side of the fence for a change.

I imagine that the Frenchman Jean-Baptiste Lafond felt much the same as he sat in the stand watching the match. Jean-Baptiste is a fine player, but he was injured and came over to see the game and support France. He arrived with a cigar of Churchillian proportions protruding from his mouth; very statesmanlike! I'm just glad he didn't blow it all over me; it is my view that if people enjoy smoke, they should go and live near the factories which belch out such filth day and night.

If I were malicious, I suppose I could say that there is a lot of hot air talked about the Five Nations Championship. It certainly isn't the greatest rugby you will ever find in the world. Part of the reason for that is the pressure to win, regardless of how you play. Risks have been all but obliterated and, given that reality, you will never see consistently high quality, entertaining and exciting rugby. You need a team which wants to win but is willing to experiment in pursuit of its goals. Believe me, a cautious, timid, error-free approach will never be enough to beat the best;

England, Scotland or anyone else will find that out, to their cost, if they play New Zealand in that way. The only hope you have against them is to attack and be bold. The French did it to Australia in the 1987 World Cup semi-final and won the day. We were extremely positive in the last Test of our 1990 series in New Zealand and won the match. But take a half-step backwards against the good teams and they will destroy you.

The Five Nations would be a great tournament to play in, from the point of view of the interest and the huge crowds everywhere you go. I would love that. But I think I would find the playing side very frustrating and not much fun at all. Great players like Lagisquet and, for many years, Underwood sometimes hardly touched the ball in entire matches and that is the ultimate indictment of the tournament.

To sum up the Five Nations as I see it, what I would really like to see in years to come is the competing teams changing the whole concept of their game and going out to play the game in the way it was meant to be played, throwing the ball around and seeing how many points they can score. Then they might find what they have had for years in terms of hidden ability; find that they can enjoy the game and discover what they have been missing out on all these years. Go and play a style of rugby like that of the Barbarians where you can have a laugh, a joke and express yourselves on the field. In a tournament like that, I think you would find that thousands of people would actually enjoy the games instead of just turning up and realising that it is going to be another 80 minutes of boring rugby.

CHAPTER
— 12 —

A DYING SPORT?

If I have ever wanted to be proved wrong about a single statement in my entire life, then it would have to be the next sentence. I am convinced that Rugby Union in Australia is a dying sport. Its demise may be slow, but it will continue steadily unless some major changes are forthcoming soon, especially on the part of the authorities.

No one can doubt my allegiance to the Union game. After all, like a great many of my former team-mates at club and international level, I could have grabbed the almighty dollar by turning professional and joining a League club. But it is my clear conviction that the future of the game in Australia is not at all bright. I do not mean the fortunes of the Wallaby team, or who will win the Sydney or Queensland Grand Final. Those events will continue to be influenced by the changing fortunes of time, just as the oceans of the world are turned into raging torrents or calm, flat surfaces by the wind. That is the way it always has been and always will be.

What is far more serious is the long-term trend in terms of the health of the sport itself. And it is in this context that I have so many fears and reservations. I look around me today and what I see hardly fills me with great optimism. Whether you are talking about Rugby Union in the ACT, New South Wales or anywhere in Queensland, the common problem relates to the professional code of Rugby League. That game is booming everywhere. Rugby Union's current position reminds me of a man gallantly but in vain trying to put out his blazing house by means of small buckets of water: damp down one area and another flares. And all the while you are losing your most precious commodity – the water itself.

Nowadays, too many youngsters in Australia are not even bothering to play Rugby Union at all. They are being snapped up directly by the League clubs, who teach them the basic skills of the professional game as kids so that they can grow into fully-fledged League players without ever really embracing the Union code. That is sad. But perhaps just as serious is the fact that Rugby Union cannot hold on to the gems it does unearth. They are gone, spirited away overnight by one of the many League clubs in Australia, and trying to replace them is simply an impossible task, given the rate of defections to professional rugby. Take the case of Ricky Stuart.

Ricky was an Australian player only fleetingly, during our tour of South America in 1986. In fact, he was never a fully-fledged Wallaby with Test caps, because the minute he had made his name as a young, up-and-coming player in Rugby Union, the League scouts were on his doorstep. In the end, before his career as a Wallaby had really begun, he had been made an offer which he simply could not refuse. His was a cruel, catastrophic loss to our game, a point I was making to anyone who cared to listen for at least two years before Stuart went with the Kangaroos on their tour of Great Britain in 1990 and virtually won the Test series single-handed. His sensational break in injury-time of the second Test, which handed Mal Meninga the winning try on a plate, was sheer quality and class. Stuart was a magnificent capture for Rugby League, but for Union the loss was incalculable.

Ricky Stuart could have been the cornerstone of the Wallaby Test side for ten years. He would have been sure to win the captaincy at some stage; he could have played half-back or first five-eighth and a side could not have had a better character around whom to put in youngsters to learn the game. His loss will continue to be felt for years to come.

So, too, will that of Michael O'Connor, who turned professional earlier in the 1980s. And there have been countless others as I have shown elsewhere in this book.

What all this adds up to is the plain fact that Rugby Union in Australia cannot afford to keep losing its best players. Nowadays, there are a few good young players coming up in Australian rugby, as the exploits of the Australian Schoolboys side have again recently shown. But no one can be under any illusion that the minute the right offer comes along, the best of those boys will be off to League. How can a sport, any sport, let alone one which is struggling badly for a toe-hold in the market in just two or three of the Australian states, ever make significant progress if that situation is to be repeated time and again?

On the 1977-78 Australian Schoolboys' tour of Britain, Wally Lewis could not even get into the Test side, such was its enormous strength in depth. I do not doubt that of those boys who toured Britain and Ireland on their 1990-91 tour, several will become outstanding first-class players. But what is the use to any game of producing numerous star players for its future if so few will eventually play a part in that future? That sport must gradually become weaker, and that is my fear for Rugby Union in Australia.

There will always be a Wallaby side, and I am sure there will be plenty of good players. But it is not the good players that make a Test side outstanding, it is the great ones. The Ricky Stuarts of this world, the Wally Lewises, Michael O'Connors and Brett Papworths. These are the people who are exceptional performers, and they are needed by Union throughout their careers, not for two or three seasons until they have fully matured and are ready to play League. Our sport cannot challenge its peers around the world if it is operating against that sort of background.

There are any number of anomalies undermining the progress of Rugby Union in Australia. I talked at the start of this book about how Rugby League was winning the battle for publicity and media attention hands-down from the Union game. That is fact, not fantasy. No better illustration of the point is available than in the ACT, where the Canberra Raiders League club have now won the premiership of the Australian Rugby League's Sydney competition for two years in succession. Winfield, the cigarette manufacturers, pump millions of dollars into their sponsorship of the sport's major competition, and no wonder – look at the vast return the company receives on its investment. The Winfield Cup is legendary throughout the world in Rugby League circles. It seems to have become almost as synonymous with Australia as hats with corks and tins of beer. Rugby League throughout the ACT has become high-profile thanks to the achievements of the Raiders club. The kids follow their exploits on television (they seem to be on so often) and naturally want to be part of it. They see guys with famous faces and well-known names. They watch the thrills and spills of a sport which is packaged extremely cleverly and make up their minds to head for League when they are old enough. Poor old Rugby Union does not get a show in the race.

Because the Canberra Raiders club has world-class players coming out of its ears – Mal Meninga, Ricky Stuart and Bradley Clyde to name just a few – they are not going to go away as a major attraction, far from it. So life can only become even more difficult for those trying to help Rugby Union prosper in ACT. How can you compete with a sport which is shown so extensively on television and fills pages and pages of newspapers and magazines? Another problem is that Rugby Union itself in ACT is no great attraction. The leading club, Canberra Royals, dominates the competition rather like Randwick has done in Sydney. The Royals undoubtedly go on to the field for some matches knowing that they are virtually certain to win, and the opposition turn up aware that a defeat is inevitable. That situation is healthy for no one, the favourites, the outsiders or the competition itself. Where is the sense of the unknown, the uncertainty which generates excitement and entertainment that will bring people to watch?

The ACT has another rugby problem which is not exclusively associated with the Canberra Raiders. Having started off with Queanbeyan and then, much later in my career, moving to the Sydney competition by joining Randwick, I have come to realise the vast difference in attitude 300 kilometres can separate. In Queanbeyan, our idea was to play the game, have a good time and make the rep. team if we could, but we never really thought very far past that. There seemed to be a lot of skills and determination missing. Players who only play for the ACT do not have an incentive to go any further. Rugby in the state has needed ACT to play New South Wales and Queensland for years and years, not just recently, as has been the case. But even with the new competition the strongest states, New South Wales and Queensland, will always win because they are at a different level of rugby.

Being brutally honest, the only factor all the states have in common is the decline in skills, and in teamwork. I do not believe Australian rugby has the foundations right, especially under its new links with the Institute of Sport. It is not the same as the system we had for years, in which well-known former players would offer their expertise. Additionally, attitudes to rugby should reflect the fact that it is an amateur sport, but when you involve a professional coaching set-up like the Australian Institute of Sport, then I believe you have taken something away from the concept of the game. As a result of the different approach, the kids coming through today have different attitudes and values. This is, of course, only to be expected to some degree as a reflection of the changes in society in general, but as regards rugby, the youngsters have been brought up in a different way and shown the game in a different light. Consequently, they end up telling us how to do it. When you tell these kids something now, there is an argument. Maybe that is the way life is going, but I believe much of this attitude derives from the Institute of Sport and its teachings. Kids seem to be grown-up at 13 now . . . or so they think. But they still have a long, long way to go. In the hands of these kids is the entire future of the game in Australia as a meaningful, potent sport.

Those in authority must address the issue of how to keep the best players in their game, rather than just sitting meekly back and watching the majority go off to League. It will be difficult and I do not profess to have all the answers but of one thing I am certain: just allowing players to pick up a couple of hundred dollars for the occasional speech at some function will not make a fig of difference. The incentives have to be a whole lot more meaningful than that. There has to be some clear, fresh direction on this front and the direction I favour is that of trust funds. Without them, I fear for the long-term future of Rugby Union in Australia.

Other factors have contrived to make many people question the wisdom of playing Rugby Union anyway. The few incidents there have been in which spinal injuries leading to paralysis have occurred have brought Rugby Union a poor press. In Australia, anything bad in Rugby Union will be publicised. League would like to nail Union down completely, probably in a wooden box, and the professional game's many supporters are everywhere, trying to do down Union. Why that is, I am not sure but it is certainly the case. It is the way the media does things in my country. Too many families have told their youngsters they are not to play Rugby Union any more in the light of some of these unfortunate accidents. They say it is too violent. Mothers watch the news and see film of violence on a rugby field and it turns them off the sport. That is why it was totally unacceptable for a guy like the Wallaby international lock Peter FitzSimons to get involved in that massive fight at the start of the first Test against France at the Sydney Football Stadium in June 1990. While Fitzie was having his own private war he was doing the game and its reputation enormous damage. Maybe in France, where he played for some years, you can get away with all that because Rugby League is not a serious alternative in that country. It is different in Australia. Test matches are tough and you want to win, but brawls like that one risk a whole lot more than just the outcome of one match. If they turn even one family away from the game, then they have been too costly.

In recent years a combination of Queensland and New South Wales players have been trying to play a particular style of rugby for the national side against a background of completely different styles at state level, creating immense friction and disharmony. If you are going to play for Australia, you have to play the same rugby. But New South Wales have a policy of running the ball whereas Queensland kick it wherever possible. If you have a Queensland five-eighth in the national side, you know for sure he will kick it, especially when under pressure, because that is what he is used to. On the other hand, a New South Wales five-eighth at No 10 in the Wallaby team will almost inevitably want to try and move the ball and the Queensland players in the side will probably feel ill at ease with such a game plan. It must make coaching the national side a nightmare.

Mark Ella hit the nail on the head when he said once that Queenslanders are like Kiwis; they just want to win, nothing else. And they don't care how they achieve it. In New South Wales, we are a bit more laid-back and want to have some pleasure out of the game. Maybe the pressures of integrating these two totally different systems have finally got to Bob Dwyer, because I think he has changed drastically from the man who coached the Wallabies for the first time back in 1982. I think Bob had become scared of failing well before 1990, and maybe the blame for that should go to the selection panel who chopped him as national coach after the 1983 tour to France. He was establishing a side then and could have gone on to enjoy the kind of success Alan Jones experienced on the 1984 trip to the UK and Ireland. But Dwyer was sacked, and when he reappeared years later, I sensed that he was always aware in the back of his mind of what might happen if his team failed. Nor could you blame him; once you have felt the knife between your shoulder-blades the thought of it must make you wince for ever after.

Bob must have known, for example, that if his team failed in the 1990 Test series against the French in Australia, he might not hang on to the job for the World Cup the following year. And for me, nothing illustrated better that pressure than the sight of Bob drinking from a bottle of Moet & Chandon after the first Test against the French last year; surely, a quite ridiculous act. We had won the first of three Tests; we could have gone on to lose the next two, and with them the series. How would the champagne have tasted then? Maybe Bob had already forgotten the lessons of 12 months earlier, when we thrashed the Lions in the first Test of a three-Test series and yet ended up losing the series 2-1. But I certainly hadn't. Bob's reaction was totally over the top. The players should have been reminded that there were two more Tests left and anything could happen. After all, it was not even half-time in the series, so to speak, and yet the bubbly was out and flowing.

I put Bob's premature celebration down entirely to the relief he must have felt to win that first match. When you consider the fact that the national coach is invariably wanted by one state and loathed by the other (it just depends which state he's from), you can understand a little of the pressure. As Australian coach, Bob Dwyer is in the middle of all this, copping the criticism with his head always on the block. So it's probably no surprise that the bloke climbed into some champagne after a Test win, but I still don't think it was the right action in the circumstances.

In 1982, when I first encountered him, Bob Dwyer was an excellent coach. He concentrated hard on the game and on our training. We trained hard and well and then we went out and put it into practice. Nowadays, however, we have as regimented a programme as an army plotting a coastal invasion. You do this and that at this or that particular time, and if you don't measure up, Bob will be there fussing and worrying that your angles of running or alignments are wrong. Eight years ago, Bob Dwyer could not have cared less about angles of running being fractionally out. He just got us mentally right for the games and we went out and played. And that is much the better way as far as I am concerned. You can overdo the preparation. Now Bob tries not to leave a blade of grass out of place on the training ground, and I put that, too, down to the massive pressure the guy must be under. I think it has reduced his effectiveness as a coach and means that we are all less likely to make a special move on the field, the unpredictable match-winning act. When you sense that your coach is under this grievous pressure, some of it starts to rub off on you, too. Those who sacked Bob in 1983 have a great deal to answer for.

I don't think Bob has been helped in his task by the fact that his assistant coach is from Queensland. Bob, coming as he does from Randwick and New South Wales, must have a completely different philosophy to Bob Templeton, a true Queenslander. I have nothing at all against Tempo, he is a heck of a nice guy and someone who has often helped me with valuable advice. It is a good idea to have an assistant to the main coach, but I would have thought the coach himself should be able to select his assistant. The pairing of Dwyer with Templeton smacks of a selection cop-out: New South Wales have their man Dwyer in, so let's balance it up with a Queenslander, Templeton. Maybe I am wide of the mark here, but I have a strong suspicion that that is the case.

Surely the assistant has to think along the same broad lines as his number one, but how can Tempo do so when Queenslanders think so differently about the game and always have done? It is a dangerous situation, for these two are very different people. It seemed an odd arrangement the day I first heard about it, and ever since I have wondered how the two can possibly integrate their views to find common ground. Given that the two states play so differently, it must be the devil of a job to find a common approach. If that is not possible, one of them has to go to the starting post not really believing in the playing pattern to be used that day. If that has ever been the case, then the whole situation has been proven as, at best, badly muddled thinking.

Rugby Union in Australia, in the World Cup year of 1991, seems to me woefully short on characters and personalities. The week I was dropped for the first Test of the 1990 series against the French in Australia, the newspapers did not seem to have anything else to write about. That cannot be right. You expect a player with so many caps to be worth some reports and comments if he loses his place, but not day after day. It was an indication that the game lacks sufficient personalities about whom to write. Nick Farr-Jones, Michael Lynagh and I are probably fairly well-known around our states; but of the rest, who has really heard much of any of them? Don't get me wrong – I do not mean that as a slur on my team-mates, just on those who write about them and sit in judgment on us all: the media. We have several people worthy of plenty of articles because they are bloody good players, but they don't get the attention they deserve. Yet when you look at Rugby League, half the nation's primary school kids could name the top 50 current League giants: Lewis, Meninga, Stuart, Clyde, Mackay, Sironen, Ettingshausen, McGaw, Elias, Roach . . . need I go on? These players are always in the limelight, always being written about and you see their photographs in every paper on a regular basis.

It is for all these reasons that I say Rugby Union is in a lot of trouble in our country. Go to a club rugby game of a good standard and the crowds are pitfully low. There is no groundswell of real support there, just the diehards. Yet 15,000 people will go and watch a boring Rugby League game between two moderate sides simply because that match has been marketed and promoted skilfully by the Rugby League authorities. It is a problem Rugby Union would do well to solve before League has the amateur code by the throat.

As for my own club rugby at Randwick, in Sydney, I have only one regret and it is something I shall take to my grave, namely, that I did not join them years earlier than I did. Randwick is an ongoing celebration of the true amateur game as it was designed to be played: with flair, spirit and style; in friendship and delight. One of the most important things about the club is the fact that every grade plays in the same style. So it is even a pleasure to watch fourth-grade rugby there because you still see some great flowing play and good skills even at that level. The obvious advantage of that is that even if the first side loses several international or top-quality players through representative calls, the club can bring in players from the second and third grades and still continue to win because the style is familiar to them all.

Training is fun, too. Jeff Sayle is a great guy. He will turn up to watch us train, rather than taking a training session and trying to cram some theory down our throats. If you do something wrong he barks at you soon enough, but he respects the fact that as we are such an experienced squad filled with internationals, we really ought to know what we are about. In essence, he trusts us and we try to repay that faith every time we go on to the field.

When I first arrived at Randwick after moving up from ACT, I could not believe what I was seeing. No regimented training programme to sweat through and suffer; no one telling international players that they had been doing it wrong for years and this was really the method to use; no one ordering us to follow certain tactics. Instead, some suggestions and guidelines were offered, but whether you wanted to take them up depended solely on yourself and your team-mates. And always there was one creed to follow: the Randwick style. It encompasses the movement of the ball, the intent to score tries rather than just to kick goals, but above all else, to enjoy what you are doing and to try to ensure that your pleasure is transmitted to those watching from the sidelines.

All very romantic stuff which might sound foolhardy to some. But the record books prove conclusively that it is perfectly possible to entertain, enjoy yourselves hugely *and* still be a winning team. The basic belief in running the ball is never sacrificed, because even when the pressure is on, we think we are more likely to score tries by running the ball than by kicking it away. We challenge the opposition to stop us running it, but very few teams achieve that. Eastwood beat us in the first semi-final of the 1989 Sydney competition because they never stopped tackling us. We then beat Easts, even though we were not playing well, and had to face them again in the Grand Final. This time, we won because we knew they could not possibly play any better than they had done in the first game against us, whereas we could do much better, and proved it.

When I went to Randwick, I had been used to the full-back role but switched to wing with the 'Galloping Greens'. Nowadays, I much prefer the full-back position; I have had enough of being left out on the wing to stand around getting cold! I like the involvement full-back offers and it gives me the chance to make decisions. I can use my kicking, and frequently do so, but a full-back also has the options before him as to whether to counter-attack. I started out in my rugby career as a full-back and played all my junior rugby, and for Queanbeyan and ACT, in that position. It was only when I was chosen for that 1982 tour of New Zealand with the Wallabies that I was switched to wing.

In recent seasons, I have found it increasingly difficult to switch from one position to the other. Your alignments are quite different and you cannot concentrate totally and exclusively on one line of thought. It never used to worry me being chosen on the wing, because with guys like Roger Gould and Glen Ella competing for the full-back slot I didn't have much chance of being picked there anyway. But when they faded from the scene, I always wanted to wear the full-back jersey, although Andrew Leeds came in and won it a few times before me.

For the non-expert, I should explain that the positions are very different. At full-back you see everything that is happening whereas on the wing you have to mark a player. At full-back you are covering the back line, whereas on the wing you must sum up the opposing player you are marking and really watch him. Preventing him from scoring is a big part of your job, as well as trying to find chinks in his own game which you can exploit when you are in possession.

I had often heard about how Randwick played, but it still took some time to get used to their style. I had never imagined how much fun it would be to play for them: all round, they are a fine club. Bob Dwyer, years and years ago when I first knew him, always used to tell me I should have one year with Randwick before my career ended. Well, I joined in 1987 and have never looked back. It must be the best club in the world. I have never seen a club where everyone drinks so much, enjoys themselves so much and plays such great rugby. When I first arrived I probably thought I was quite smart, but I was soon put in my place. It was made clear to me very quickly that I was not a star, even if my ego insisted otherwise; I was not special, and nor was anyone else in the team. I was just another player, like Mark Ella, Simon Poidevin, John Maxwell and all the others. In fact, it was not even a coach or fellow player who laid down the Randwick rules to me but a young lady in the clubhouse one evening. I was enchanted as she went right through me, giving me a really hard time as she pointed out all this to me, but I was grateful for the lesson. It extended the Randwick legend, and I soon learned that thinking about your mates and helping the team was what counted, not your own ambitions or desires on the field. You enjoyed the game, sure, that was the fundamental part of it all, but you also went out there with a responsibility to ensure that your mates around you got pleasure out of it all too. You do not think of yourself at Randwick but of the guys in the side with you.

I cannot think of another club in the world I would rather play for than Randwick. Bath, the top English club, asked me to play for them for a year a little while back but I wasn't interested. Pierre Berbizier, who is with the French club Agen, also asked me whether I would go there a few years ago, but the answer was the same: sorry, mate, I'm with the best club side in the world, so why would I want to go anywhere else? Midway through the winter of the 1990-91 season, while I was in Italy, an Australian journalist rang up one day and asked me if rumours linking me with Drummoyne, the newly-promoted club in the Sydney competition, were true. Well, that was a story of pure invention, like so many others. I would never leave Randwick willingly. It would feel like a betrayal of Sayler, and I could never consider that!

Ever since I joined them, I have felt privileged to have an allegience to Randwick. They are renowned the world over for their outstanding qualities and it is fabulous to be a member of such a club. You feel a deep association, wherever you go, with them. Perhaps a good example of the differing attitudes this creates compared to those of players from other clubs occurred in 1989, around the time of the climax to the Sydney premiership competition. Eastwood, as I mentioned earlier, were going well that year and reached the first semi-final where they beat us. When we met them in the Grand Final they were without a key member of their side, the Wallaby wing Ian Williams.

Ian had decided to take up an invitation to join the World XV on tour in South Africa at that time. He left his club in limboland when, in my view, he should have been in Australia representing them. You owe loyalty to your club, and I don't think it is fair to clear off and play somewhere else just when they need you most. Others could perhaps have gone but didn't, and I believe that Ian made the wrong decision in leaving at that particular time. Your club helps to make you what you are and you should never forget that. I don't think you can repay that assistance over the years if you go abroad when the Grand Final is imminent. You should at least show loyalty to your club-mates: what they thought about having to play Randwick without Ian in their side I am not sure, but I can hazard a guess.

The whole issue of South Africa is such an emotive one that I have, almost deliberately, put off dealing with it here until the very last moment. It is not that I have no knowledge of the place; I went there in 1985 for the Natal Sevens tournament, and found it a very interesting country. But I feel ill-equipped to make the kind of comment on South Africa's fortunes and principles that some might expect from me. I am no politician, just a humble sportsman, and I don't see it as my place to analyse and criticise a country and its politics just because I happen to be used to something else.

I will confine my thoughts to a few personal experiences from the time I was there. In Durban, I saw an elderly white lady walk into the hotel where we were staying, past a black porter who had opened the door specifically for her. She swept through without a word of thanks or anything. Charming, what manners, I remember thinking at the time, and don't let anyone ever try and tell you that the blacks are uncouth. You could read the derision that woman felt for an ordinary guy like him, just as clearly as you could read a newspaper. People like that turn me right off, I can't handle them. I walk away because I just want to be rude to them. That woman, by her arrogance and unpleasantness, put me off a lot of white people in South Africa.

Let me be open and say here and now that I would go to South Africa to play rugby again. I had the chance a couple of years ago but declined because it was not convenient. Those who choose not to go to South Africa on principle may very well be genuine, thoroughly decent people adhering to the demands of their consciences. But they should perhaps also remember that South Africa isn't the only nation on earth with a record of maltreating its black population. We in Australia do not exactly treat the Aborigines nicely and the Americans have dealt with their black people like rubbish. There are, too, a few skeletons rattling around the Poms' cupboards in terms of the way black people have been kept back in Britain.

Yet who are the world's greatest runners and many of its best singers? Which is the best cricket team in the world? Black people and a black side, the West Indians. So isn't it about time the world awoke to the fact that so many of these people have so much to offer? By contrast, isn't it clear that so many white people around the world seem to like the life of drunkards and layabouts? I am not surprised a section of the whites in South Africa are spitting fury at the reforms of President de Klerk. They don't want to be ruled by black people the way they have ruled them these past years.

Andrew Slack's Wallaby side should have gone to South Africa but, for a variety of reasons, the tour was abandoned at the eleventh hour. Some saw the hand of Alan Jones behind that because it no longer suited him to let us go there. Others said that certain people within South Africa had gone cold on the idea of a tour. I wonder if we will ever know the truth. What had been clear was that we would all make quite a sum of money from the projected tour. The exact details of the deal I can no longer remember, but I do know it was worth more than $100,000 to each player, much more, in some cases, with sums being paid into offshore accounts ready to be used after retirement. But the whole thing fizzled out anyway, so it is irrelevant. The money would have come in handy, but money isn't everything in life. Had I not wanted to go for moral reasons, a million bucks wouldn't have got me there. But I liked the idea of a very successful Australian Wallaby side, one of the best the country had ever known, taking on the Springboks to see who really was the best in the world. The challenge seemed fascinating, and it was a pity when the tour collapsed.

The subject of South Africa has been covered at such length elsewhere that I don't feel I can add to the arguments here, except to say that I am sure South Africa will be back in the international fold before very long.

In writing this book, I have tried to avoid falling through the trap-door of predictability. I have wanted to explain something of my life and my thoughts, rather than to produce a long, drawn-out reproduction of all the matches I ever played in, all the tries I ever scored and all the players I came across. Such attention to detail, padded with tales of the subject doing this, that and the other and proving what an absolutely brilliant bloke he has always been, bores me to death. It has been my intention to get well away from all that and I hope that aim has been fulfilled.

However, if anyone wants to accuse me of predictability, I will now give them some excuse by running through a mythical 'best Australian team of my time' – the side I would most like to have played in. This might be an exercise in futility, but it does give me the opportunity to select and highlight some of the best players I have known during my time in the game. My choice is confined to Australians for the simple reason that I have played with or against them most and feel in a position to pass informed comment on them. Others from around the world I have not seen enough to know well.

My best full-back would be Roger Gould. He was one of the greatest, a colossus who, although often bothered by injury, was a fantastic player when fit and firing on all cylinders. He was very big, could kick a ball like a mule and was totally safe and confident under the high ball. His physique alone commanded respect and you could rely on Roger. Two other full-backs of recent times have, I suppose, generated certain comparisons. Serge Blanco and myself are, however, different players. Maybe both of us are more unpredictable than Roger ever was, but you couldn't rely on Serge and I under the high ball the way you could on Roger Gould. With Roger, you never had that feeling of uncertainty. And when he went forward into the line, it would normally take two or three defenders to stop and hold him so that in the meantime openings appeared elsewhere due to his intervention. This was a major factor in our success on the 1984 Grand Slam tour of the UK and Ireland.

On the wing, I would go for Brendan Moon, assuming I also had a place in this mythical XV! Maybe some people failed to see all his great attributes. He didn't finish a world record try-scorer and he never made his name like Lynagh and Papworth did in Australian rugby. But those who knew him recognised Moonie for what he was: a truly dependable wing who always did supremely well at what he did attempt. You looked at Brendan in the way a householder looks at an insurance policy; he was there, a protection especially in times of difficulty. He was not the fastest bloke I have ever known off a standing start, but once into his stride, he was devilishly hard to bring down.

My centres would be Michael O'Connor and Michael Hawker. What a pair of creative backs, players who had it all between them – speed, flair, vision, timing and pure class. They had quite different characteristics but when they came together, which was only fleetingly, because of Michael O'Connor's departure to Rugby League, they looked superb. However small the space, they could create room for those around them. I have talked before about Michael O'Connor's tremendous qualities, so let me try to describe Hawker. He was a player's player. He might not look terribly exciting in the way of a Papworth, but he was very strong and adept at putting others into space. He was a subtle player with fine ball skills who could hold the ball up. Perhaps he lacked the ability to really motor with the ball in his hands, and under pressure he became known for kicking. But, playing for Sydney University, he probably got into that habit. I would not say he had the many skills of O'Connor but he complemented him brilliantly.

I wouldn't have to think too long and hard about my choice for the first five-eighth position. Mark Ella is, in my opinion, the best rugby player I have ever known or seen. Why? Just the way he played, the manner in which he could release others and turn up in the unlikeliest of positions or places simply because of his telepathic reading of a game. Nothing worried Mark, and his skills were unbelievable. Even years after his apparent retirement from top-class rugby, his skills remained of a high quality. He was always a great thinker on the game but opponents could never legislate for Ella, because he would suddenly do something no other player in the world could even think of achieving.

Nick Farr-Jones would be my half-back. He was lucky enough to play inside Mark Ella on that 1984 Grand Slam tour. What an education for Nick, so early in his career! Since then, he has developed into the world's finest half-back; a very good player with a super pass who thinks quickly, is brave and determined and can read a game so well. He has a real go in attack, and although I think we saw Nick at his best before he was made captain, he remains to this day a player out of the very top drawer.

As for the forwards, hard cheese! If you think I am going to discuss in public the merits of tight heads and tight flankers and breakaways and hookers, then you have another think coming! I'll leave all that technical stuff to someone else. But of the players who have worn the Wallaby jersey in my era, I don't think I would look too much further than the 1984 Grand Slam pack which made such an outstanding contribution to our triumph. A front row of McIntyre, Lawton and Rodriguez could hold its own against any side anywhere, while the locks, Steven Cutler and Steve Williams, won us a heap of line-out ball. My best back row would be Steve Tuynman at No 8 with Simon Poidevin and David Codey on the flanks.

It is no coincidence most of those players were together on that 1984 tour to Britain and Ireland. In many ways, that was the finest Wallaby side I ever had the privilege to play in, although our achievement in beating the All Blacks in New Zealand two years later may have been marginally the better success.

I could go on forever with stories of great days, mythical teams and of the marvellous times I have known in the game. Rugby Union has been and remains my life, and when I am finally forced to retire, I shall experience a void which I wonder whether I shall ever manage to fill. It has been a great time, a marvellous experience, and I've made friends to last a lifetime. It has taught me so much; about myself, about others and about life itself. I could have asked for no more from any sport. When the time comes for me to hang up my boots, I won't be thinking of all the caps I have won, the matches in which I have played or the tries I scored for Australia. Certainly, all those mean a great deal to me, but anyone who plays Rugby Union will understand that two factors stand head and shoulders above all others in this great game: the friends you make along the way and the pleasure you have gained simply from participating. You don't have to represent the Wallabies to find that pleasure, it is there just as much in the Extra B XVs on Saturday afternoons throughout the world. And to share that pleasure in your sport, to make further friends around the globe, you can go into any rugby club anywhere in the world and it is as though this common delight which is Rugby Union football just embraces you. I cannot think of any other sport which would have offered me or anyone else of my time so much. For that, I shall always be deeply grateful.